D1221244

Understanding World History

The Digital Age

Harry Henderson

Bruno Leone
Series Consultant

ReferencePoint Press®

San Diego, CA

With thanks to Lori Shein for the opportunity
to write about one of my favorite subjects.

© 2013 ReferencePoint Press, Inc.
Printed in the United States

For more information, contact:
ReferencePoint Press, Inc.
PO Box 27779
San Diego, CA 92198
www. ReferencePointPress.com

LIBRARY OF CONGRESS CATALOGING-IN-PUBLICATION DATA

Henderson, Harry, 1951-
  The digital age / by Harry Henderson.
     pages cm. -- (Understanding world history series)
  Includes bibliographical references and index.
  Audience: Grades 9 to 12.
  ISBN-13: 978-1-60152-482-9 (hardback)
  ISBN-10: 1-60152-482-X (hardback)
  1. Information technology--History--Juvenile literature. 2. Information society--Juvenile literature. I. Title.
  T58.5.H478 2013
  303.48'3309--dc23

                                                                    2012026168

Contents

Foreword

When the Puritans first emigrated from England to America in 1630, they believed that their journey was blessed by a covenant between themselves and God. By the terms of that covenant they agreed to establish a community in the New World dedicated to what they believed was the true Christian faith. God, in turn, would reward their fidelity by making certain that they and their descendants would always experience his protection and enjoy material prosperity. Moreover, the Lord guaranteed that their land would be seen as a shining beacon—or in their words, a "city upon a hill,"—which the rest of the world would view with admiration and respect. By embracing this notion that God could and would shower his favor and special blessings upon them, the Puritans were adopting the providential philosophy of history—meaning that history is the unfolding of a plan established or guided by a higher intelligence.

The concept of intercession by a divine power is only one of many explanations of the driving forces of world history. Historians and philosophers alike have subscribed to numerous other ideas. For example, the ancient Greeks and Romans argued that history is cyclical. Nations and civilizations, according to these ancients of the Western world, rise and fall in unpredictable cycles; the only certainty is that these cycles will persist throughout an endless future. The German historian Oswald Spengler (1880–1936) echoed the ancients to some degree in his controversial study *The Decline of the West.* Spengler asserted that all civilizations inevitably pass through stages comparable to the life span of a person: childhood, youth, adulthood, old age, and, eventually, death. As the title of his work implies, Western civilization is currently entering its final stage.

Joining those who see purpose and direction in history are thinkers who completely reject the idea of meaning or certainty. Rather, they reason that since there are far too many random and unseen factors at work on the earth, historians would be unwise to endorse historical predictability of any type. Warfare (both nuclear and conventional), plagues, earthquakes, tsunamis, meteor showers, and other catastrophic world-changing events have loomed large throughout history and prehistory. In his essay "A Free Man's Worship," philosopher and mathematician Bertrand Russell (1872–1970) supported this argument, which many refer to as the nihilist or chaos theory of history. According to Russell, history follows no preordained path. Rather, the earth itself and all life on earth resulted from, as Russell describes it, an "accidental collocation of atoms." Based on this premise, he pessimistically concluded that all human achievement will eventually be "buried beneath the debris of a universe in ruins."

Whether history does or does not have an underlying purpose, historians, journalists, and countless others have nonetheless left behind a record of human activity tracing back nearly 6,000 years. From the dawn of the great ancient Near Eastern civilizations of Mesopotamia and Egypt to the modern economic and military behemoths China and the United States, humanity's deeds and misdeeds have been and continue to be monitored and recorded. The distinguished British scholar Arnold Toynbee (1889–1975), in his widely acclaimed twelve-volume work entitled *A Study of History,* studied twenty-one different civilizations that have passed through history's pages. He noted with certainty that others would follow.

In the final analysis, the academic and journalistic worlds mostly regard history as a record and explanation of past events. From a more practical perspective, history represents a sequence of building blocks—cultural, technological, military, and political—ready to be utilized and enhanced or maligned and perverted by the present. What that means is that all societies—whether advanced civilizations or preliterate tribal cultures—leave a legacy for succeeding generations to either embrace or disregard.

Recognizing the richness and fullness of history, the ReferencePoint Press Understanding World History series fosters an evaluation and interpretation of history and its influence on later generations. Each volume in the series approaches its subject chronologically and topically, with specific focus on nations, periods, or pivotal events. Primary and secondary source quotations are included, along with complete source notes and suggestions for further research.

Moreover, the series reflects the truism that the key to understanding the present frequently lies in the past. With that in mind, each series title concludes with a legacy chapter that highlights the bonds between past and present and, more important, demonstrates that world history is a continuum of peoples and ideas, sometimes hidden but there nonetheless, waiting to be discovered by those who choose to look.

Important Events of the Digital Age

1830s
Charles Babbage designs (but never completes) the Analytical Engine, a mechanical, programmable computer using punched cards.

1936
Alan Turing's theoretical "universal computer" suggests the power of automatic computation.

1951
Eckert and Mauchly introduce UNIVAC, the first commercially available computer.

1850 / 1940 1950 1960 1970

1890
Herman Hollerith's punched-card tabulator is used in the US census. It evolves into IBM's office technology.

1952
IBM enters and soon dominates the commercial computer market.

1969
ARPANET begins with four machines; it will eventually become the Internet.

1943
World War II rages; Colossus electronic computers speed the breaking of German codes.

1960
The DEC PDP-1 introduces minicomputers, which are more compact and cheaper than mainframes.

1946
ENIAC, designed by J. Presper Eckert and John Mauchly, goes into operation. It has more than eighteen thousand vacuum tubes.

1977
The Apple II and other microcomputers begin the personal computer (PC) revolution.

2006
Mark Zuckerberg launches Facebook.

1985
Microsoft Windows 1.0 is released. Later versions will come to dominate the PC desktop.

2004
Google dominates web searching; its stock soars.

1981
The IBM PC is introduced, using a DOS operating system from Microsoft. It will become an industry standard.

1994
Netscape and Amazon begin web-based businesses; eBay follows the next year.

2012
Microsoft introduces Windows 8 and enters the tablet market.

1980 **1990** **2000** **2010**

1984
A Super Bowl commercial introduces Apple's Macintosh. It will introduce graphical user interfaces to PC users.

2007
Apple's iPhone introduces a new generation of smart phones. Twitter becomes popular.

2010
Tablet computers such as Apple's iPad begin to challenge laptops.

1991
Tim Berners-Lee introduces the World Wide Web.

The Defining Characteristics of the Digital Age

In little more than half a century, the electronic digital computer has profoundly transformed science, industry, business, and society itself. In changing how people organize their work and lives, the developments of the digital age can be compared to the Industrial Revolution that began during the late eighteenth century.

Starting around 1750, the development of steam-driven industry and, later, transportation, had profound effects. There was a massive movement of people from farms to growing cities. Vast new empires, particularly the British Empire, drew upon raw materials from distant lands to feed textile and steel mills. Factory-made clothing and furniture changed how people looked and lived. Natural gas and electricity greatly improved lighting, heating, and cooking. Railway trains and steamships spanned oceans and continents in days rather than months. The ability to mass-produce newspapers and books changed the way people learned about the world.

Webs of Communication

As the industrial age was changing the material circumstances of life, it also began to change communications and social relations. When words started zipping through telegraph wires, life itself seemed to be accelerating at an electrifying pace that disturbed many thoughtful people.

In his 1854 book *Walden, or Life in the Woods*, American writer Henry David Thoreau complained, "We do not ride on the railroad; it rides upon us." As for the newly introduced telegraph, Thoreau observed, "We are in great haste to construct a magnetic telegraph from Maine to Texas; but Maine and Texas, it may be, have nothing important to communicate."[1]

As seems to be the case with each new technology, the skeptics are readily answered by the enthusiasts. The early American novelist Nathaniel Hawthorne, whose fiction expressed many important themes of American life, has a character who remarks on the telegraph:

"By means of electricity, the world of matter has become a great nerve, vibrating thousands of miles in a breathless point of time. . . . Rather, the round globe is a vast head, a brain, instinct with intelligence! Or,

The Industrial Revolution brought life-changing inventions such as the telegraph, the steam engine, and the railroad (all pictured in this hand-colored lithograph from 1876). In similar fashion, the digital age has profoundly transformed science, industry, business, and daily life.

shall we say, it is itself a thought, nothing but thought, and no longer the substance which we deemed it!"[2]

The global "brain" that Hawthorne saw in the telegraph in 1851 would become truly pervasive more than a century later when computers began to use the worldwide communications network. The vision of ideas spreading around the world in a few hours would become reality as the World Wide Web grew during the 1990s and 2000s. Nevertheless, thoughtful observers today continue the debate begun by Thoreau, Hawthorne, and others who lived during the earlier industrial and communications revolutions.

Technology as Powerful Ideas

In his essay "Five Things We Need to Know About Technological Change," cultural critic Neil Postman observes that "embedded in every technology there is a powerful idea, sometimes two or three powerful ideas. These ideas are often hidden from our view because they are of a somewhat abstract nature. But this should not be taken to mean that they do not have practical consequences." Postman goes on to suggest that the consequences of technological change reach deep into people's personal and social lives: "Every technology has a philosophy which is given expression in how the technology makes people use their minds, in what it makes us do with our bodies, in how it codifies the world, in which of our senses it amplifies, in which of our emotional and intellectual tendencies it disregards."[3]

Consider how the cell phone (and particularly the smart phone) has changed how people relate to one another and to their world. Today people are always connected, but that means they are always reachable. Absolute privacy and solitude become rare—and something that must be consciously planned. The connection to one's text messages, Twitter feed, or e-mail sometimes feels like a sixth sense. For many people, being deprived of that connection feels like suddenly becoming deaf or blind.

Postman also notes that new forms of technology and media (which today are really the same phenomena) never change only one thing. By shaping the lens through which people view the world, they eventually change everything.

Rapid Change

Unlike the steam engine or the locomotive, the computer is not one machine but many. The same sort of software and hardware that brought the rover *Curiosity* to the surface of Mars in 2012 also can be used for the more controversial purpose of killing enemies in the hills of Pakistan with remotely piloted drones. Meanwhile, a tablet computer can now serve as slate, navigation device, television remote, security monitor, or home controller. The combination of the computer's mastery of the web of communications and its programmable versatility continually drives the expansion of the digital age into virtually every aspect of modern life.

A striking characteristic of the digital age is the speed of innovation and development. The Industrial Revolution was felt to be abrupt at the time, but it still took generations to have its full effect. Even as late as the years between 1960 and 1990—when profound social changes were occurring around the world—the everyday forms of communication, transportation, and entertainment saw little change.

Between 1995 and 2010, however, an entire marketplace and social arena sprung into existence, signified by names such as Amazon, Google, Facebook, and several devices whose names begin with the letter *i*. Mobile devices now keep people continually connected, and information on just about any topic is only a click away. In this pervasive, always-on world, new services and applications now emerge in a matter of months rather than years—and sometimes fade away just as quickly.

Evolution or Revolution?

How is one to understand such rapid change? Is it continuous evolution or a sudden revolution? Evolution usually brings to mind Darwinian natural selection, resulting in a gradual change in the anatomy or behavior of organisms. However, observers such as science-fiction

In the digital age, people are nearly always connected and reachable thanks to computers, tablets, cell phones, e-mail, and social networks. The technology of the digital age has influenced human interaction on a global scale.

writer Vernor Vinge have noted that technology, acting on human culture, promotes evolution at a much faster pace:

> Animals can adapt to problems and make inventions, but often no faster than natural selection can do its work—the world acts as its own simulator in the case of natural selection. We humans have the ability to internalize the world and conduct "what if's" in our heads; we can solve many problems thousands of times faster than natural selection. Now, by creating the means to execute those simulations at much higher speeds, we are entering a regime as radically different from our human past as we humans are from the lower animals.[4]

According to veteran technology writer Kevin Kelly, the comparison of technological evolution to animal evolution is particularly apt because technology as a whole (which he calls the "technium") has many of the characteristics of living organisms, including autonomous behavior and self-directed growth:

> The technium wants what we design it to want and what we try to direct it to do. But in addition to those drives, the technium has its own wants. It wants to sort itself out, to self-assemble into hierarchical levels, just as most large, deeply interconnected systems do. The technium also wants what every living system wants: to perpetuate itself, to keep itself going. And as it grows, those inherent wants are growing in complexity and force.[5]

Kelly is not suggesting that computers or technology as a whole are currently conscious of intentions or desires in the way people are. What he is saying is that people have invented technology, but technology also tends to reinvent us. A smart phone or a Facebook page seems to grab at human attention and channel it in certain directions.

Kelly thus focuses on how technology can drive social developments. However, technological breakthroughs also depend on broader historical developments. For example, the desperate struggle between the Allies and the Nazis during World War II spurred the development of the first computers. The machines were needed because modern weapons were becoming too complicated to design by hand. Perhaps the best way to understand the relationship between the development of technology and the events of history is that they spur each other—and at an increasing pace.

Chapter 1

What Conditions Led to the Digital Age?

Like all great developments in world history, the digital age has no single cause and did not come into existence all at once. It depended on earlier technological developments, such as electrical engineering and electronics. It was also a response to the needs of scientists and engineers to perform lengthy calculations and government departments and corporations to manage the information generated by a complex industrial society. Ultimately it would be the urgent need to solve wartime challenges that would give birth to the first electronic computers.

A Need for Numbers

By the early nineteenth century Britain's worldwide empire depended on reliable ocean navigation—and that required tables of numbers to aid in calculating positions. Other tables were needed to calculate insurance risks, interest on investments, and statistics needed by government planners. Charles Babbage, a British mathematician and inventor, once recalled that as a young student he was sitting in the library daydreaming, a book of logarithms open in front of him. Someone asked him what he was dreaming about, and he replied, "I am thinking that all these tables might be calculated by machinery."[6]

Babbage eventually designed two computing machines—the Difference Engine and the more ambitious and programmable Analytical

Engine. Neither device was actually built, and Babbage's work largely was forgotten for more than a century. Gradually, hand-operated mechanical calculators appeared in offices, but by the 1930s, when engineers had to design such things as automatic telephone exchanges and fighter planes, computational capacity was falling well behind the pace of technological development.

The Information Challenge

The other challenge of managing the modern world had to do with the ever-expanding flood of information. The problem of how to keep tabs on a modern industrial economy came to a head for the US census. In 1880, with a national population nearing 50 million people, the government had to hire fifteen hundred clerks to collect and tabulate the census reports. The process took so long that the director of

Charles Babbage designed the world's first automatic computing engines but never built them. The first complete Babbage engine, Difference Engine No. 2 (pictured), was built to the inventor's original specifications and completed in London in 1991.

statistics, John S. Billings, worried that the next census would not be completed in time to be useful. He suggested to one of his staff members, Herman Hollerith, that some form of mechanical tabulation might be employed for the 1890 count.

Hollerith thought about how railroad conductors punched holes in different parts of a train ticket to identify a passenger and prevent fraudulent use. Similarly, he concluded, cards could be punched by census takers to record information about people, such as gender, age, and occupation. He then designed a machine that used metal rods and mercury-filled electrical contacts to register a signal for each place where a hole was punched. Electromagnetic counters would then move dials to tally the number of cards that had a given characteristic.

Hollerith's card tabulator was a remarkable success. About 60 million cards were tallied, completing the 1890 census count in only two and a half years rather than taking a decade or more. Hollerith established a company to manufacture and sell his tabulator machines to businesses. After passing through a few changes in ownership, the technology became a key product for a company called the International Business Machines Corporation (IBM).

New Ideas in Computing

By the 1930s Hollerith's simple tabulator had morphed into a variety of devices that could be linked together to tabulate, sort, and calculate totals from punched cards. A typical insurance office, for example, might have a whole room filled with such machines, together with desk calculators, all operated by an army of clerks amid a din of clattering and the ringing of bells.

Such a scene was a far cry from the quiet offices or lecture rooms where mathematicians chalked their equations on blackboards. However, the leap from mechanical calculator to all-purpose electronic computer would owe much to mathematicians and their rather abstract concerns. Mathematics had developed in astonishing ways during the nineteenth and early twentieth centuries. There were new kinds of geometry with curved space (very useful for Albert Einstein's theory of

Charles Babbage and the Steam Computer

As a boy, Charles Babbage (1791–1871) showed both mechanical and mathematical ability. He went on to become an expert in calculus and a member of Britain's scientific Royal Society at the age of twenty-five. Dismayed by the inaccuracy of hand-compiled mathematical tables, Babbage considered how to build a calculator that could use a repetitive procedure (now known as an algorithm) to generate such tables automatically. Unfortunately, Babbage was not a very good manager, and he and his workers failed to meet the challenge of creating the thousands of mechanical parts that were needed.

In 1836 Babbage noted a remarkable new idea in his notebook:

This day I had for the first time a general but very indistinct conception of making an engine work out *algebraic* developments—I mean without any reference to the *value* of the [symbols]. My notion is that the cards (Jacquards) of the calc. engine direct a series of operations and then recommence with the first, so that it might be possible to cause the same cards to punch others equivalent to any number of repetitions.

Although fully mechanical, the engine (perhaps driven by steam) would have worked much like a modern computer. Instructions and data would have been fed in on punched cards, calculations would have been done in a mill (similar to today's central processing unit), and results would have been stored in a memory called a store.

In 1991 the Science Museum in London completed a full working replica of the Difference Engine. In 2011 a new project began work on a replica of Babbage's Analytical Engine.

Quoted in Anthony Hyman, *Charles Babbage: Pioneer of the Computer*. Princeton, NJ: Princeton University Press, 1985, p. 244.

relativity) and the discovery that there was more than one kind of infinity. There was also the systematic study of logic and the structure of mathematics itself. This latter discipline had led to the question of the limits of calculation. What kinds of problems could be solved? How could you tell whether a given problem had a solution?

A brilliant, if rather awkward, young British mathematician named Alan Turing tackled this problem. As a result, the idea of the universal computer was born. In his 1936 paper "On Computable Numbers," Turing created an imaginary device that would become known as the Turing machine. It was something like a typewriter that had an endless paper tape that was divided into little squares. Each square could have a symbol printed in it, or it could be blank. (These two possibilities are often represented by the numbers one and zero). The typewriter could be ordered to move the tape one space forward or back or to write or erase the symbol, depending on what was already in the square. Turing showed how even complex calculations could be performed by giving the machine the appropriate instructions.

Turing and a few others quickly grasped the significance of this theoretical result. If anything could be calculated by giving instructions to a Turing machine, then it should be possible to build an actual machine that could automatically and rapidly carry out such a program. The actual physical embodiment of the one and zero of the Turing machine could be represented by switches that could either be on (one) or off (zero). Future computer scientist Claude Shannon at Bell Labs realized that ideas described by nineteenth-century British mathematician George Boole could be applied to the on/off of switches, noting that "it is possible to perform complex mathematical operations by means of relay circuits. Numbers may be represented by the positions of relays and stepping switches. Interconnections between sets of relays can be made to represent various mathematical operations."[7]

Over time, electrical or electronic calculators using these principles would probably have gradually begun to find their way into offices. However, the development of digital computing technology would be drastically accelerated by the outbreak of a new kind of war.

The Secret Battle of World War II

When World War II began in Europe in 1939, the conflict soon spread to the Atlantic Ocean, where German U-boats (submarines) tried to sink the ships bringing supplies and soldiers to Great Britain. To secure their radio transmissions, the Germans used a particularly advanced electromechanical coding machine called Enigma. The machine used a series of wheels, or rotors, containing switches for each letter of the alphabet. In addition, the machine had a series of plugs that could be connected to scramble the code even further. The Germans believed that because the machine had so many possible settings, no enemy could decode their signals.

Unknown to the Germans, the Enigma machine had been reverse engineered—that is, re-created by studying the patterns in the cipher it created. Mathematicians and other code breakers were using methods devised by Alan Turing to statistically analyze Enigma messages, aided in part by the careless practices of some German operators. (Operators tended to use the same phrases over and over, such as "nothing unusual to report" or even "Heil Hitler").

The code breakers looked for these common phrases, called cribs. If they suspected a crib was in a particular location in the message, they could try possible settings that might turn the cipher text into the crib text. Because the Enigma design was such that no letter could be encoded as itself (that is, an *e* in the cipher text could not be represented by an *e* in the decoded text), any setting that produced such a result could be eliminated.

Even when narrowed down in that way, there were too many possibilities for a solution to be worked out by hand. The code breakers began to tackle the problem by building mechanical rotor decoding machines, called bombes, which could quickly go through the possible combinations. However, when the Germans added extra rotors to their Enigma, the British bombes could no longer keep up.

Under the leadership of a British engineer named Tommy Flowers, the mechanical bombes were replaced by electronic machines that used vacuum tube logic circuits and a high-speed tape reader that could

World War II accelerated the development of digital computing technology as engineers and others working for the Allies reverse engineered the German electromechanical coding machine, Enigma (pictured), in hopes of breaking coded messages. These efforts ultimately led to the first electronic digital computers.

eventually process code characters at the rate of twenty-five thousand per second. These machines, called Colossus, although designed for a specialized purpose, were arguably the first electronic digital computers.

The Mark I

Meanwhile, an American electrical engineer named Howard Aiken had begun working on a calculating machine. In a 1937 memo, Aiken described a "Proposed Automatic Calculating Machine" consisting of "a switchboard on which are mounted various pieces of calculating machine apparatus. Each panel of the switchboard is given over to definite mathematical operations."[8]

Receiving funding and design and engineering help from IBM's president, Thomas J. Watson Sr., the Mark I (also known as the IBM Automatic Sequence Controlled Calculator) was completed in 1943 at Harvard University at a cost of about half a million dollars. The machine stood 8 feet (2m) high and stretched for 51 feet (16m), though it was only 2 feet (61cm) thick. The Mark I was a programmable computer, but it was not electronic. Its innards consisted of 730,000 separate parts—including elaborate electromechanical switches, relays, and counters—all driven by drive shafts connected to a four-horsepower motor. Data was entered by flipping switches for each digit, and instructions were read from punched paper tape. It could multiply two twenty-three-digit decimal numbers in about six seconds. This was slow by modern electronic standards, but impressive for a mechanical device.

ENIAC

While the Mark I was being constructed at Harvard, a rather different computing machine was being secretly built at the University of Pennsylvania. In August 1942 physicist John Mauchly had written a memo on "The Use of High-Speed Vacuum Tube Devices for Calculating." Joined by an engineer, J. Presper Eckert, their proposal was accepted by the Ballistic Research Laboratory of the US Army.

The eventual result was the Electronic Numerical Integrator and Computer (ENIAC), a monstrous machine that filled a large room with cabinets containing about eighteen thousand vacuum tubes. Looking back in 1961, computer historian Martin H. Weik summarized the significance of ENIAC for the development of the digital age: "ENIAC was the prototype from which most other modern computers evolved. It embodied almost all the components and concepts of today's high-speed, electronic digital computers."[9]

Although the war was over by the time ENIAC was ready in November 1945, it was quickly put to work on calculations to determine the feasibility of a hydrogen bomb design. The program revealed that the design was flawed, a calculation that researchers said could not even have been attempted without the computer. Within months, ENIAC's existence became public knowledge. On February 14, 1946, ENIAC's wartime secrecy was lifted during a dramatic press conference. As mathematician Arthur Burks later recalled, "I explained what was to be done and pushed the button for it to be done. One of the first things I did was to add 5,000 numbers together. . . . The ENIAC added 5,000 numbers together in one second. The problem was finished before the reporters looked up!"[10]

A New Form of Intelligence?

While the general public marveled at the performance of ENIAC, Alan Turing was looking to what the machines of the future might accomplish. In a 1950 paper, Turing predicted that "at the end of the century the use of words and general educated opinion will have altered so much that one will be able to speak of machines thinking without expecting to be contradicted."[11]

The idea of intelligent machines began to find its way into the popular media. Following World War II, popular magazines featured many exciting new technologies. These included jet planes, radar, nuclear energy, television, and the computer, which was often called an electronic brain. Actually, the memory units in computers are not connected in the same way as the neurons that make up human brains and do not work the same way. Despite attempts by experts and some journalists to correct such misconceptions, they would persist. One historian notes that following the press conference that made ENIAC public, "anthropomorphic references in headlines continued to shape the public perception of computers for years to come. ENIAC was referred to as a child, a mathematical Frankenstein, a mechanical Einstein, a whiz kid, a predictor and controller of weather, and a wizard."[12]

Although speculation about what computers might do someday was exciting, the number of computers in existence in the late 1940s could literally be counted on the fingers of one hand. If computers were actually to become part of everyday life, people would have to find practical uses for such exotic and expensive machines. They would have to create an industry.

Computer operators of the 1940s program the massive ENIAC by plugging and unplugging cables and adjusting switches. ENIAC technology formed the basis of many of the components and concepts that have made possible the modern high-speed, electronic digital computer.

UNIVAC and the Birth of an Industry

In 1948 Howard Aiken, developer of the Mark I calculator, believed that the nation needed perhaps half a dozen computers, mainly for scientific research. He did not believe there would be a commercial market for the machines. The feats of calculation attributed to machines such as ENIAC amazed the public, but it was not immediately obvious how computers could be used to process the kind of data that flowed through the business world, such as data used to make payrolls, perform accounting, or keep track of inventory.

ENIAC designers Eckert and Mauchly were not among those doubting the value or usefulness of electronic computers. They were willing to bet their careers that computers could be sold for business and general-purpose data processing. When administrators at the University of Pennsylvania demanded that they sign over any future patent royalties, they refused, resigned their faculty positions, and went into business for themselves.

In 1947 they incorporated as the Eckert-Mauchly Computer Corporation (later acquired by Remington Rand). As they began to contact businesses that they hoped would be interested in buying computers, they did get some expressions of interest. Within about a year their potential customers included the military, a number of prominent aircraft companies, and the Prudential and Metropolitan insurance companies, which were struggling to manage millions of policyholders.

Eckert and Mauchly offered the Universal Automatic Computer, better known as UNIVAC, in 1951. UNIVAC got some free publicity when it was used to predict the winner of the November 1952 presidential election. When the computer first suggested an overwhelming victory for Republican Dwight Eisenhower over Democrat Adlai Stevenson, CBS television officials rejected the results and made the programmers tinker with the program to make the election seem closer. (When Eisenhower actually beat Stevenson by an overwhelming margin, the network executives had to admit the computer had been right the first time.)

By 1954 about twenty UNIVACs had been sold, each for about half a million dollars. Despite UNIVAC's central processor using five thousand vacuum tubes, some of which could burn out at any time, the machines proved remarkably reliable. Indeed, in 1953 the US Census Bureau reported, "We never encountered an incorrect solution to a problem which we were sure resulted from an internal computer error."[13]

The UNIVAC provided working memory for one thousand twelve-digit numbers or characters. Data was encoded in electrical pulses that were put through a transducer and sent as relatively slow-moving waves through a cylinder filled with mercury, from which they could be retrieved or refreshed as needed. For external data storage, UNIVAC gained speed by using magnetic tape instead of punched cards.

Getting Down to Business

Particularly in business, people began to think of computers not as glorified calculators but as information-processing machines. UNIVACs were put to work for the US Air Force to manage the flow of military supplies, and one found its way to the Lawrence Livermore Laboratory to do classified nuclear weapons research.

A model for future business data processing was established by General Electric (GE), which obtained its UNIVAC for payroll, inventory control, order processing, and billing. However, Roddy Osborn, the consultant who had recommended that GE invest in a computer, believed that general-purpose computers such as UNIVAC offered businesses more than just fast, efficient handling of processes. He believed that computer programs could be used to analyze production processes, improve scheduling, minimize excess inventory, and even analyze the needs and desires of customers and forecast sales levels. Osborn noted, "While scientists and engineers have been wide-awake in making progress with these remarkable tools, business, like Rip Van Winkle, has been asleep. GE's installation of a UNIVAC may be Rip Van Business's first 'blink.'"[14]

Imagining the Future

The popular imagination, however, was somewhat conflicted about what a computerized future might be like. On the one hand, computers seemed to be ushering in a world of effortless automation, providing low-cost goods for everyone, not to mention abundant leisure. On the other hand, many workers in the United States and other industrialized nations saw prosperity as the hard-won fruit of the struggles of the labor movement. What would happen if the new computers and other automated machinery meant that one person could do the work of five or ten?

Experts also disagreed about the impact of computers and automatic machinery, and the debate continued through the 1950s and 1960s. In 1963 economist Yale Brozen suggested that "perhaps the gains of the automation revolution will carry us on from a mass democracy to a mass aristocracy. . . . The common man will become a university educated world traveler with a summer place in the country, enjoying such leisure-time activities as sailing and concert going."[15]

Designing the Modern Computer

Alan Turing had shown that his imaginary machine could solve any computable problem once the logic rules and starting conditions were specified. Actual computers, however, had to use real electronic circuits to represent and manipulate the data. In the first computers, such as ENIAC, this meant setting numerous switches to the appropriate one or zero values before a new program could be run.

Working independently during the later 1940s, John von Neumann in the United States and a group of British researchers at the University of Manchester developed a way to store program instructions directly in a computer's memory along with the data to be processed. This design became known as the von Neumann architecture, and it is found in nearly all computers used today.

To run a program, the control unit fetches a program instruction from memory. The instruction is sent to the arithmetic logic unit, which in turn may fetch data from another part of memory, perform a computation or comparison, and send or store the result. The control unit then processes the next instruction, and so on. However, because the program remains in memory, it can include an instruction to jump back to a previous part of the program and repeat a series of operations, creating a loop. Such loops and logic branches allow programs to change their behavior based on the contents of data or the results of previous calculations.

At the other extreme, Norbert Wiener, a noted mathematician and the developer of cybernetics (the study of control and feedback in complex systems), expressed misgivings about the new technology in an influential 1954 book. "It is perfectly clear," he wrote, "that this will produce an unemployment situation, in comparison with which the present recession and even the depression of the thirties will seem a pleasant joke."[16]

A related concern was that the ability to understand and use computers would create a new elite class. Another writer, Donald Michael, suggested that "most of our citizens will be unable to understand the cybernated world in which they live. . . . There will be a small, almost separate, society of people in rapport with the advanced computers. . . . Those with the talent for the work probably will have to develop it from childhood and will be trained as intensively as the classical ballerina."[17]

The Future of Employment

Looking back over half a century, one sees that the terms of the debate have shifted, but many of the concerns expressed by these early commentators remain. Optimists argue that although workers may be temporarily displaced by machines, computers have also created vast new industries—electronics manufacturing, software, and, more recently, web-based businesses. Displaced workers should be offered training so they can enter these new job markets. Young people in particular should be given an education that will equip them for a rapidly changing future.

Pessimists, however, believe it is unrealistic to think that millions of former assembly-line workers (who used to make good wages) can be retrained to become computer programmers or website designers. Instead, they are likely to be forced into lower-paying jobs in the service sector, such as clerks or janitors.

Ironically, the debate over automation has been overtaken in recent years by a new fear—not of computers or robots, but of millions of workers in China, India, and other countries who are being trained to perform not only low-skilled jobs but also highly technical ones, and for much lower pay. Thus, the dreams and fears stirred by the first mainframe computers remain alive today, though in a somewhat different form.

Even as people struggled to understand how computers were beginning to change their world, the technology itself was developing rapidly. IBM, an old company with a new mission, would usher in the era of the mainframe computer.

Chapter 2

Mighty Mainframes

Computers steadily improved during the 1950s. They gained greater memory capacity, faster access to data, and more powerful processors. Improvements in memory and storage systems would be key to providing the data-processing capacity needed for business. The reliability and utility of the machines would enable the computer industry to grow and prosper.

Even today most computers have at least two kinds of memory. Working memory (often called random access memory, or RAM) needs to be as fast as possible in order to provide the data immediately needed for processing. The other kind of memory, sometimes called mass storage, does not need to be as fast, but it must be able to store large amounts of data, such as a file of payroll records. Data from this slower memory can be read and stored in the faster working memory as it is needed.

Faster Memory and Storage

One early form of fast memory used cathode-ray tubes (found until recently in televisions and computer monitors). Using beams of electrons to store data rather than display pictures, the tubes were fast but had limited capacity (the equivalent of about a paragraph of text.) They were also bulky and frequently unreliable.

A new form of fast, reliable working memory—called core memory— was introduced during the mid-1950s. A magnetic core consists of an array of many tiny donut-shaped pieces of magnetic material embedded in a grid of wires. Any one of these pieces could be magnetized in one of two directions (representing the numbers *1* or *0*) or sensed (read) by sending an electrical signal through the appropriate wires. Core memory became the standard high-speed computer memory from the mid-1950s well into the 1970s, when it was replaced by integrated-circuit chips.

Besides better working memory, computers also gained new forms of mass data storage. Magnetic tape had been used since the early 1950s to store large data files. Improved tape drive designs allowed tapes to be read and positioned more quickly, but tape had an inherent disadvantage. In order to read a particular data record from a tape, the tape must be mechanically advanced to that particular position. Thus, tapes were best used for reading entire files or programs at a time, but the amount read was limited by the amount of memory available.

A different kind of magnetic recording was developed to solve this problem. It came first in the form of a large rotating drum, but in 1956 IBM introduced the disk drive, which remains a common form of storage today. The disk drive consists of a stack of rotating platters coated with a substance that retains magnetism. Data can be written or read by means of magnetic heads that ride above the platter on a cushion of air. With a disk drive, data can be stored or retrieved at any location simply by repositioning the magnetic head.

Computer designers also sought to make processing more efficient. Because the central processing unit (CPU) that did the calculations used electronic tubes, it was much faster than magnetic tapes or even disks. Often during processing, the CPU would have to switch over to controlling the tape or disk drive to read a new batch of data. However, IBM developed a separate device, called a channel, that could take over control of peripheral devices, freeing the CPU to resume calculations.

IBM Enters the Computer Industry

By the mid-twentieth century IBM had dominated the office machine market for more than a generation. IBM electric typewriters, calculators, tabulators, and other business machines were in widespread use. However, the company did see the threat represented by UNI-VAC, and in 1952 it announced its own general-purpose computer, the IBM 701.

IBM and UNIVAC did not have the early computer industry entirely to themselves. Honeywell became a significant player, and General Electric's ERMA computer was also a successful entry and inaugurated a major new market: banking. By the 1950s banks were struggling with the need to process a growing number of checks, a task that involved armies of clerks examining them, determining the account they were drawn on, and verifying the amount. Bank of America, using an ERMA system and special magnetic printing on its checks, could automatically read the account numbers, encoded check amounts, and routing information. Other companies, including some in Great Britain and Europe, experienced some success, especially in niche markets like factory automation. Nevertheless, by the 1960s most users, particularly those in business, considered the term *computer* to be synonymous with *IBM*.

Computers in the Cold War

The 1950s was a time of growing prosperity for many Americans, but it was also a time of Cold War fears. Both the United States and the Soviet Union stockpiled nuclear weapons and developed faster bombers to deliver them. During this period, military planners faced a new technological threat. How could the air defenses detect, track, and target enemy bombers that might be traveling at jet speeds and carrying nuclear bombs?

A young electrical engineer named Jay W. Forrester at the Massachusetts Institute of Technology (MIT) was placed in charge of an ambitious project called the Semi-Automatic Ground Environment (SAGE), which was intended to link a vast network of ground and ship-based radars via radio and telephone links. The data would be processed in regional centers using powerful computers called Whirlwinds. Eventually IBM built thirty SAGE systems for the military, each with two computers to provide backup if one failed. The system would remain in place until 1983.

Besides demonstrating that reliable large-scale computers could be built, SAGE provided a major boost to developments that would become key to computing in coming decades. These included an early form of computer networking, text displays, even graphics, and new forms of user interfaces.

IBM Rules the Mainframe World

The 1960s began with IBM in the driver's seat of the computer industry. Business executives and office managers were familiar with IBM as a maker of the office equipment that had been used throughout much of the century. To this name recognition and existing business relationships, IBM added a large group of sales and service representatives specifically for computers.

A company buying or leasing an IBM computer would receive a visit from a representative knowledgeable about the customer's line of

A glassblower makes cathode-ray tubes for televisions in 1955. Although bulky and frequently unreliable, these tubes made possible an early form of fast computer memory.

business. IBM developed and sold most of the software applications for its machines, and it even provided training. If something went wrong with an IBM computer, technicians would quickly arrive to find and fix the problem. This full-service philosophy made IBM equipment more expensive than similar products, but it reassured users that they were buying a complete and reliable data-processing solution.

By the mid-1960s IBM controlled about three-quarters of the worldwide computer market. The April 1964 introduction of the IBM System/360 (S/360) solidified IBM's dominant position in the world computer market. The S/360 was actually a line of upwardly compatible machines and peripheral devices that could be mixed and matched as users' requirements changed. Rather than being sold outright, systems could be rented starting at about $2,700 per month and ranging up to $115,000 for a multisystem configuration.

The S/360 series was the most successful large computer in history. Within a month of its introduction, eleven hundred machines were on order. One of the S/360's designers, Steve Will, would later comment that "few products in American history have had the massive impact of the IBM System/360—on technology, on the way the world works or on the organization that created them."[18]

IBM would become known to both admirers and critics for its corporate culture, which seemed to typify the mainstream conformity of 1950s America. According to Roddy Osborn's history of the mainframe era, for IBM,

loyalty to the firm was a virtue above all others. . . . The business was like a football team, with [IBM president] Tom Watson—a strikingly handsome man, with a penetrating gaze—as both coach and cheerleader. Techniques were developed to reinforce the employee's devotion to Tom Watson. There was the emphasis on dark suits and white shirts; THINK signs hung on office walls; employees sang company songs (one lyric went: "Our voices swell in admiration; Of T.J. Watson proudly sing; He'll ever be our inspiration; To him our voices loudly ring."[19]

Developments in Programming

All the advances in computer hardware during the 1950s and 1960s would have been of little use without comparable advances in the art of programming. In the early days, programs had to be written in machine language, which consisted of cryptic codes that told the computer to perform an operation and provided the addresses (locations) for data retrieval and storage. Although a step up from ENIAC's plugs and switches, machine-language programming was quite tedious.

The development of an assembler program that could translate labels into machine addresses helped somewhat, but noted computer scientist John Backus later recalled that programming in the early 1950s

> was a black art, a private arcane matter involving only a programmer, a problem, a computer, and perhaps a small library of subroutines, and a primitive assembly program. Existing programs for similar problems were unreadable and hence could not be adapted to new uses. General programming principles were largely nonexistent. Thus each problem required a unique beginning at square one, and the success of a program depended primarily on the programmer's private techniques and invention.[20]

What was needed was a way for the computer to translate programs that were written in a more readable language into the necessary machine instructions. Grace Hopper, a US Navy admiral and computer programmer, became the leader in developing such programs, called compilers. In 1952 she introduced A-0, which was a compiler for UNIVAC; it was soon followed by improved versions. Hopper used the term *automatic programming* to describe how programs could be created automatically from a description given in a natural-looking language.

FORTRAN and COBOL

The early compilers and assemblers made programming easier, but it was still far from simple. By the mid-1950s business managers and scientists wanted to be able to create their own programs without having to master arcane languages. Meanwhile, professional programmers were faced with the task of keeping track of programs that could consist of many thousands of lines of instructions. They, too, needed computer languages that were easier to understand. These demands led to the development of the first widely used higher-level programming languages: FORTRAN and COBOL.

FORTRAN (formula translation) would be designed primarily for mathematical work. To be useful for mathematicians, the language would have to be flexible enough to specify commonly used mathematical expressions and operations. At the same time, the language compiler would have to be efficient enough to work well with the available computer memory and processors. John Backus identified the key problem: "Can a machine translate a sufficiently rich mathematical language into a sufficiently economical program at a sufficiently low cost to make the whole affair feasible?"[21]

The Soviet Union puts on a massive arms display in Red Square in 1957. The US and Soviet weapons buildup of the Cold War inspired the development of powerful computers for military use.

Working with Mainframe Computers

Unlike today's computers, running a mainframe computer during the 1950s and 1960s required much more than just clicking on or touching an icon. Along the walls of a mainframe computer room, the various modules of the computer were mounted on metal frames (hence, the name *mainframe*) inside cabinets. The central processor was usually in a separate cabinet. It consisted of circuit boards to which were soldered thousands of individual transistors and other components.

Sitting down at the operator's console, one would find a typewriter-style keyboard and numerous status lights. An experienced operator could use the patterns of lights to read the data values currently stored in the processor and even use switches to make corrections.

The other immediately noticeable feature of the classic mainframe installation would be a row of cabinets containing large spinning reels of magnetic tape. Before running a program, the operator would have to obtain the required reels from the tape library and mount them so the computer could read the data.

Until the 1970s the program itself would be loaded by feeding a deck of punched cards into the card reader. The deck would begin with instructions that would identify the program as a batch and specify the specific computer resources (such as tape drives) to be used. These cards would be followed by the cards containing program instructions.

In 1993 the National Academy of Engineering would give Backus the prestigious Draper Prize for developing FORTRAN, which was introduced in 1957. The academy described FORTRAN as "the first general-purpose, high-level computer language."[22] FORTRAN quickly became a hit with scientists, engineers, and other mathematically oriented users.

FORTRAN was ideal for programs that consisted mostly of calculations. Business applications, on the other hand, usually involved applying a small amount of calculation to large amounts of data. The initiative to create a higher-level computer language for general business applications was promoted by the US Department of Defense, which had to deal with numerous government contractors and their different computer systems and software.

Hopper was in a good position to respond to this challenge. She had already been working toward the goal of a programming language similar to English. In an interview years later, Hopper noted that the computer is "basically a symbolic manipulator. When it's doing numerical calculations, it is manipulating arithmetic symbols, and when it's doing data processing, it's manipulating data processing symbols."[23]

By 1960 a committee had laid out the specifications for COBOL, or the common business oriented language. COBOL inherited much of its structure from Hopper's pioneering compilers. COBOL statements read almost like real English sentences. For example, instead of using cryptic variables such as "IF HW > MH," a COBOL statement would begin, "IF HOURS-WORKED IS GREATER THAN MAXIMUM-HOURS." In the following decades tens of millions of lines of COBOL code would power applications in business and government.

The 1950s had seen the computer industry come of age. Computers were getting faster, and they could store and process larger amounts of data. Thanks to new programming languages such as FORTRAN and COBOL, scientists, engineers, and particularly businesspeople could have software tailored to their needs. The mainframe would be the workhorse of computing for many years to come, but already new kinds of computers were emerging, and they would be used in new ways.

From Tubes to Transistors

As the art of programming continued to develop, another revolution in computer hardware was developing. By the late 1950s computer designers seeking faster and more compact machines were facing a fundamental problem. Even though the machines now had faster memory

The IBM System/360, introduced in 1964, solidified IBM's dominance in the world computer market. The S/360 series of computers was the most successful large computer in history.

and storage systems, the central processor—the part of the computer that actually computes and carries out other logic operations—still consisted of bulky and somewhat unreliable vacuum tubes.

In 1947 John Bardeen, Walter Brattain, and William Shockley, working at Bell Labs, developed the first practical transistor (an achievement that would earn them the 1956 Nobel Prize in Physics). Transistors use semiconducting solid materials (such as germanium) that can perform the same functions as vacuum tubes but take much less space, use less power, and run more reliably. The IBM 1401, introduced in 1959, was an early and successful transistorized computer; more than ten thousand 1401s were eventually sold.

Transistors and Minicomputers

By the 1960s transistors and more-compact circuit boards were being used to make mainframes more powerful, reliable, and somewhat smaller. But the new kind of hardware could also be used to make computers that were much smaller than mainframes and considerably cheaper. These machines became known as minicomputers.

The Digital Equipment Corporation (DEC) would come to be the dominant minicomputer company, starting with its introduction of the PDP-1 in 1960. DEC's users, being sophisticated computer scientists, engineers, and students, took a much more hands-on approach to their use of computers than was typical in the mainframe world. They frequently tinkered with them, wrote their own software, even created new operating systems. Rather than try to control how their machines were used, DEC actively encouraged innovations. If someone suggested an improvement in the design or wrote a better piece of software, DEC was likely to adopt it, or it would be maintained by the users themselves.

Although the PDP-1 was only a modest commercial success, by 1965 DEC had sold more than fifty thousand PDP-8 systems. The PDP-8 used a faster type of transistor and was designed with plug-in modules that were both versatile and easy to service.

Changing Uses for Computers

The development of the minicomputer made computers accessible to many universities and smaller companies that could not afford a mainframe machine. Another factor that would make computers more accessible was the development of new operating systems that would

Imagining Computer Applications

The idea of using a computer to automate data processing occurred to many government officials, scientists, engineers, and business executives starting in the 1950s. However, developing such applications required not only imagination but also a considerable investment of money and time.

In some cases—such as the US census or the processing of Social Security payments—the advantages of automation were clear. Although processing such large amounts of data would be a challenge, the existing formats and procedures offered guidance for what was needed.

Other applications, particularly in science and engineering, were more challenging. Writing programs that could simulate the behavior of neutrons in a nuclear reactor or the flow of air over an airplane wing required both a deep understanding of physics and the ability to create ways to visualize the results of the calculations. Even more complex was a field such as meteorology, where the accuracy of weather forecasts depended on the variables considered and the accuracy of the data gathered and input.

Sometimes innovative applications sprung from unlikely sources. Around 1950, Lyons, a large British chain of restaurants and tea shops, sent its managers to America to observe the operation of EDVAC (a more advanced version of ENIAC). Lyons decided to build its own computer, called the Lyons Electronic Office (LEO). LEO's software could handle payroll, inventory, distribution and delivery to shops, and detailed management reports. Lyons eventually offered its data-processing services to other British companies, pioneering the electronic data processing service industry.

allow the machines to be shared by more than one program and more than one user.

The first computers did not need much of an operating system. They could run only one program at a time. While running, the program had access to all of the computer's memory and other resources. Because many programs did not actually use the full capacity of an expensive mainframe machine, this way of using computers was wasteful and inefficient. In the 1960s computer designers began to develop operating systems that could allow two or more programs to use the same computer at the same time. This would increase the amount of work a computer could do and reduce the cost of running a given program.

Multitasking, as it came to be known, required the development of more sophisticated operating systems. The system had to keep track of the portion of memory used by each program and ensure that programs did not trespass into other programs' territory. Because the computer normally only had a single CPU, the processing also had to be allocated among the running programs.

In addition to running more programs at a time, there was also the possibility of letting more than one user share the computer. An early multiuser system was the Compatible Time-Sharing System (CTSS), which was running at the Massachusetts Institute of Technology by 1962. With multiple users also came the need to create and manage an account for each user and to provide a space for storing files. Thus, the idea of organizing files into directories or folders was born.

Time-sharing systems meant that more people could have direct access to computers, making programming easier to learn and more satisfying. Students in colleges and even some high schools could be remotely connected to a computer and run their programs interactively. They were aided by the Beginner's All-Purpose Symbolic Instruction Code (BASIC), developed at Dartmouth College during the mid-1960s. Minicomputers—and the culture that developed around their users—were beginning to broaden the horizons for computer use. The 1970s would bring new hardware and new possibilities.

Chapter 3

Computers Get Personal

The history of any technology has two strands: one technical and one human. For a new development to arise, the state of the art must advance to the point where an innovation is practicable. Without adequate metalworking technology, for instance, ideas for steam engines could not have progressed. Likewise, it is equally important for people to have the imagination to see how new devices might be used. As contemporary software developers point out, there must be at least one "killer app"—a useful application that will make people want to buy the new technology. This philosophy, which is employed with smart phone advances today, was also at work in the development of personal computers during the 1980s.

From Transistors to the Microprocessor

The state of the art in computer circuitry was developing rapidly during the 1960s and 1970s. Early transistorized systems used individual transistors wired to printed circuit boards on which the necessary connections were already stamped. The next step was the integrated circuit (IC), which was first demonstrated by Jack Kilby, an engineer at Texas Instruments, in 1958. Kilby would be awarded the Nobel Prize in Physics in 2000 for the theory underlying this device. Robert Noyce of Fairchild Semiconductor independently developed a different version that was easier to manufacture.

Instead of using a printed circuit board, the IC deposits the transistors and other components themselves (in the form of material with

The Original Hackers

During the late 1950s and 1960s a computing counterculture began to develop among students at places such as the Massachusetts Institute of Technology and Stanford University. Unlike mainframes, the minicomputers favored by these students could be used interactively by typing commands at a typewriter-like terminal. Some of the young programmers became obsessed with working on the computer, coming in late at night when the machine was not being used by the regular users. They began to call themselves *hackers* because they hacked at a system until they figured out how to get it to do what they wanted.

According to Steven Levy, who tells their story in his book *Hackers*, there was a set of common beliefs and practices shared by the otherwise individualistic hackers. Information (software and documentation) should be freely available to be shared, not restricted or sold. Computers and other tools or devices should always be fully accessible. Bureaucracies of any sort are obstacles to be ignored if possible and otherwise worked around. Finally, authority and credibility come only from the quality of one's contribution— the code you could write, and the interesting new things you could make a computer do. Today many people think of the hacker as a criminal who creates viruses or steals information. However, the original idea of the hacker can still be found at companies such as Google, which encourages employees to spend a portion of their work time pursuing their own ideas for new applications.

appropriate properties) onto a small chip, typically made of silicon. Although the first IC chips contained only a few dozen transistors, by the mid-1970s large-scale integration had been achieved, with tens of thousands of transistors on a single chip. (Today chips can have tens of billions of transistors.)

In 1969 a Japanese manufacturer asked Ted Hoff of Intel to design a powerful desk calculator. As a result, Hoff came up with the idea of putting all of the components of a fully functional computer—including the CPU, data registers, and microcode program—onto a single chip. Hoff would later note that "the real key is not necessarily the number of components or the number of features, but the organization, the architectural concept in which you take a general-purpose computer and build it into a system."[24] Together with several other engineers, Hoff developed the Intel 4004, which was the first microprocessor, or computer on a chip. By the later 1970s Intel and other companies, such as Zilog and Motorola, were making microprocessors, and newer models could work with larger chunks of data (eight bits—ones or zeroes—at a time instead of only four).

Homebrew Computers

For the personal computer (PC) revolution to begin, the availability of exciting new devices like the microprocessor had to come together with a community of sophisticated experimenters and tinkerers. It happened that conditions for this development were particularly ripe on the peninsula south of San Francisco. This area would become known as Silicon Valley, deriving its name from the basic element used in computer chips.

Nearby Stanford University proved to have a strong, formative influence on the development of this advanced electronics industry. Stanford faculty members worked closely with entrepreneurs to create such technology companies as Hewlett-Packard and, more recently, Google. Other organizations and companies that helped this incubation of technology were the US Department of Defense and military contractors, particularly aviation companies such as Lockheed. Funding for the miniaturized electronics technology needed to develop satellites and spacecraft during the space race of the late 1950s and 1960s proved to be a boon for civilian applications, including computing and communications technology.

The availability of technical training, good jobs, and surplus parts encouraged college students (and sometimes dropouts) to tinker with transistors and logic circuits. When the first microprocessors became available, a number of such inventors realized that it would be possible to develop the small, inexpensive machines that would become known as microcomputers.

In 1975 two of these tinkerers, Gordon French and Fred Moore, started a group called the Homebrew Computer Club. It was located in the heart of Silicon Valley in an area known as Menlo Park. Steve Wozniak, a member who went on to design the Apple II computer, recalled the early meetings:

"The theme of the club was 'Give to help others.' Each session began with a 'mapping period,' when people would get up one by one and speak about some item of interest, a rumor, and have a discussion. Somebody would say, 'I've got a new part,' or somebody else would say he had some new data or ask if anybody had a certain kind of teletype."[25] The individualistic, creative, yet cooperative spirit of the Homebrew Computer Club, coupled with the availability of exciting new technology, made conditions ripe for invention and entrepreneurship.

Computer in a Kit

Meanwhile, in a garage in Albuquerque, New Mexico, two electronics engineers named Ed Roberts and Forrest Mims III began thinking about building a computer kit using a new processor, the Intel 8080. Art Salzberg, editor of the hobbyist magazine *Popular Electronics*, encouraged Roberts and Mims to turn their ideas into a working computer in an enclosure literally the size of a breadbox. The machine, called the Altair 8800, appeared on the cover of the magazine's January 1975 issue.

Programming the Altair involved flipping switches to represent the binary digits (ones and zeroes) that signified each instruction, hitting a switch to enter the instruction, and repeating the process dozens of times—a tedious process reminiscent of ENIAC. Programming received a bit of a boost when a version of the easy-to-use BASIC language was developed by another young enthusiast named Bill Gates. In 1975 Gates had formed a company that he called Micro-Soft. He was concerned that his company was losing out to the free flow of ideas that was common among computer enthusiasts. Gates complained in a 1976 open letter in the *Homebrew Computer Club Newsletter* that people were copying the BASIC tapes and giving them away, depriving the company of any return for its efforts: "As the majority of hobbyists must be aware, most of you steal your software. Hardware must be paid for, but software is something to share. Who cares if the people who worked on it get paid?"[26]

Jobs, Wozniak, and the Apple II

In 1976 two Homebrew members, Steve Wozniak and a friend named Steve Jobs, decided they could build a computer and market it to fellow enthusiasts through a new company they called Apple Computer. They called their machine the Apple I and sold it for the unusual price of $666.66. Unlike the Altair, the Apple contained a fully assembled circuit board, but to do anything with it, the user still had to supply a case, power supply, keyboard, and video display.

This first machine was clearly aimed at the technically minded, but in 1977 Apple introduced a more refined—and more expensive— offering, the Apple II. The Apple II came in a sleek case with a built-in keyboard and was ready to be hooked up to a video monitor or (with the aid of a converter) an ordinary television set. Business writer and journalist Robert Slater notes that "the $1,350.00 Apple II weighed twelve pounds and it was easy to use. It became known as the Volkswagen of computers. It was the first finished product, the first computer one could buy ready-made—no longer did one have to buy a kit and put a computer together."[27]

Another Apple innovation was the inclusion of empty slots inside the case. These slots had standard connectors for adding boards that could expand the memory (up to sixty-four kilobytes), interface the machine to a printer, and even run alternative operating systems or programming languages. The machine came with a simple version of the BASIC computer language built in, and programs could be stored on or loaded from an ordinary cassette tape recorder. (A floppy disk drive, and eventually a hard disk drive, came a bit later.)

Steve Jobs, cofounder of Apple Computer, introduces the Apple II computer in 1977. The Apple II weighted twelve pounds and was easy to use. It was also the first ready-made computer that did not come as a kit to be built by the purchaser.

The Apple II was the most successful of the first generation of personal computers. Other machines from Commodore (PET and C64) and Radio Shack (TRS-80) as well as British products such as the Sinclair ZX80 and the BBC Micro also became popular, particularly with hobbyists and young people eager to experiment with programming—particularly games.

Personal Computers and Business

The question of the usefulness of computers—which first had been asked in the early 1950s—would be repeated for the new desktop computers of the early 1980s. The machines were certainly not powerful enough to replace mainframes for doing payroll or inventory. However, people in offices needed to create documents, spreadsheets, and maybe a chart or two. They needed business applications that would run on the new desktop machines.

Such applications soon began to appear. Dan Bricklin and Bob Frankston, business administration graduate students at Harvard, were experienced programmers. One day while tediously working through a class assignment with pencil and calculator, it occurred to Bricklin that a program that could calculate and quickly update spreadsheets would be a compelling use for PCs. The result was VisiCalc, introduced in 1979 for the Apple II. In just one year the program was selling at the rate of twelve thousand copies a month at a price of $150 each.

The other basic office task, word processing, existed by the 1970s in the form of dedicated systems involving advanced electric typewriters with limited editing and built-in correction features. By the mid-1970s word processing systems by IBM, DEC, and particularly Wang included video screens so pages of text could be viewed page by page and scrolled through. These machines were expensive, typically costing around ten thousand dollars.

When the Apple II and other microcomputers became available, developers began to create programs that could be used to edit text and perform at least some of the functions of dedicated word-processing machines. In the 1980s several programs came into wide use: WordStar, WordPerfect, and, later, Microsoft Word. A two-thousand-dollar Apple II, which could both do spreadsheets and replace a ten-thousand-dollar word-processing unit, was beginning to look like a bargain.

The Standard PC

As new software began to prove the utility of the microcomputer in the office, a battle began over what system and architecture would become

The small but increasingly capable machines were becoming a part of many offices. However, the growing number of people who had to learn how to use the machines also served to highlight a problem. The PCs of the early 1980s were not easy to use. Each program had a different system of menus and commands to be mastered. Furthermore, even basic tasks such as finding or copying files relied on arcane commands that had to be typed exactly at a command prompt.

In 1979 Apple's Steve Jobs visited the Xerox Palo Alto Research Center (PARC). Like the Bell telephone company, Xerox had given researchers funding and free rein to develop new ideas in computing, without necessarily expecting immediate commercial benefit. In 1972 Xerox PARC researchers developed a prototype desktop computer called the Alto. The machine had a high-resolution display that showed graphical fonts instead of simple characters. Along with it came individual program windows, menus, and icons. These objects could be selected using the mouse, a pointing device that had been invented by Douglas Engelbart back in 1963.

In addition to what Jobs saw at Xerox PARC, he was also getting ideas from two talented Apple designers. Back in 1967 Jef Raskin had written a computer-science thesis that advocated the use of an all-graphic user interface, and Bill Atkinson had already designed software using pull-down menus and the ability to drag objects across the screen.

The combination of pointing device and graphical user interface (GUI) was not just an innovation in hardware. It represented a new model for thinking about computing. With a GUI, the computer screen simulated a desktop—a familiar object to any office worker. In 1982 David Smith, a developer of the Star (the Alto's commercial version), noted that

> every user's initial view of the Star is the Desktop, which resembles the top of an office desk, together with surrounding furniture and equipment. It represents a working environment, where projects and accessible resources reside. On the screen are displayed pictures of familiar office objects, such as documents, folders, file drawers, in-baskets, and out-baskets. These objects are displayed as small pictures, or icons.[29]

The significance of the GUI can be demonstrated simply by the fact that today everything from desktops down to cell phones use icons. But while the ideas being developed at Xerox PARC were spreading through the computer-science world, Xerox's Star was expensive (costing at least sixteen thousand dollars) and was not being effectively marketed.

Meanwhile, Steve Jobs and Apple were looking for a successor to the Apple II that could compete with or even leap over the more powerful IBM PC. They used what they were learning about new user interfaces to design what would become a very different kind of PC. Apple's first attempt, a machine called the Lisa, was both expensive and incompatible with both the Apple II and the PC clones; thus, it did not sell well. Despite this failure, Jobs was undeterred. He put together a new team and had it work on a smaller, boxlike machine with the screen built in—the Apple Macintosh (Mac).

The Battle for the Desktop: Mac Versus Windows

In January 1984 a dramatic commercial aired during the Super Bowl. It opened with a long tunnel filled with drone-like workers watched over by wall screens. Suddenly, a woman wearing track clothes and carrying a hammer, pursued by sinister police officers, raced toward the central screen, which showed a depiction recalling Big Brother from George Orwell's *1984*. The woman hurled the hammer at the screen, causing it to shatter. A final voice intoned, "On January 24, Apple Computer will introduce Macintosh. And you'll see why 1984 won't be like *1984*."[30]

The commercial, directed by Ridley Scott (later known for his movies *Blade Runner* and *Alien*), would find its way into advertising history. It was perhaps the opening shot in a decades-long battle over design and marketing philosophy between Apple and the PC manufacturers.

Computer historian Paul Ceruzzi notes that "the Mac's elegant system software was its greatest accomplishment. It displayed a combination of aesthetic beauty and practical engineering that is extremely rare."[31] The first Mac models were still relatively expensive, and their limited memory, floppy disk drive, and processing power were taxed by the demands of the graphical interface. However, subsequent models became a popular favorite in applications such as desktop publishing and photo and video editing.

It took some time, but Bill Gates and Microsoft knew they had to respond to the Mac's innovative user interface with something that could run on the IBM PC and its clones. Fueled by the revenue from selling millions of copies of MS-DOS as well as a growing presence in office software, Microsoft could undertake the development of a new operating system—Microsoft Windows. Windows 1.0, released in 1985, was balky and poorly received by users. When Windows 3.0 was released in 1990, it proved to work much more smoothly and had the capacity to use the growing amount of memory available in PCs (now

In 2001 Microsoft's Bill Gates (right) and Intel's Andy Grove celebrate the twentieth anniversary of the IBM PC. The IBM 5150 PC, the company's first personal computer, is on the far right. On the far left is another historic PC, this one built by Compaq. In between the two older computers are examples of modern laptops.

measured in megabytes rather than kilobytes) and faster processors to run multiple programs effectively.

More powerful machines with more memory arrived quickly in the highly competitive PC market. This power in turn allowed for more complex software, such as Microsoft Office, an integrated program that offered word processing, spreadsheets, databases, and other functions with an ever-growing array of features. By the 1990s it seemed Microsoft was close to achieving the company's original goal (usually attributed to Bill Gates) of "a computer on every desk and in every home, running Microsoft software."[32] However, a new arena was becoming increasingly important—networking, the Internet, and the World Wide Web.

Chapter 4

A Connected World

As computers became more common, computer scientists, engineers, and ordinary users began to consider how the machines could be linked together into networks to provide even more processing capability and access to data. Once computer networks were built, it was soon discovered that they could also be used to help people communicate and coordinate their efforts.

Using Computers to Communicate

By the 1960s trying to program a major project required learning and sharing more and more information. At places like universities, users of minicomputer systems needed to know about bugs, workarounds, new versions of operating systems, and new tools like program editors. Computers were supposed to be good at storing and retrieving information, so why not use the computer itself as a sort of bulletin board for exchanging ideas and spreading news?

Sometime around 1969 Ken Thompson and Dennis Ritchie began to develop what would become the popular and influential Unix operating system. Later Ritchie would note, "What we wanted to preserve was not just a good environment in which to do programming, but a system around which a fellowship could form. We knew from experience that the essence of communal computing, as supplied by remote-access, time-shared machines, is not just to type programs into a terminal instead of a keypunch, but to encourage close communication."[33]

Once time-sharing made it possible for many people to use the same machine, a rudimentary form of online communication was possible. Files could be posted where everyone could access them, and people could update them with information about new developments. People could also use a central file to let individuals know they had posted a file with a message for them—a very rudimentary form of e-mail.

Lawrence Roberts, an important contributor to the development of computer networking, noted that these facilities, primitive by today's standards, had already begun to change how computer users saw their relationship with one another and with the system: "As soon as the time-sharing system became usable, these people began to know one another, share a lot of information, and ask of one another, 'How do I use this? Where do I find that?' It was really phenomenal to see this computer become a medium that stimulated the formation of a human community."[34]

Bulletin Boards and Online Services

Most PC users of the 1980s did not have access to Unix systems and networks, which were limited mainly to university students and scientists. However, in 1978 two microcomputer enthusiasts, Ward Christensen and Randy Suess, created the first hardware for running a computer bulletin board system. Users could log in by having their computer dial the appropriate phone number using a device called a modem. Once connected, users could read and post messages on various topics and share games and utility programs.

These early bulletin board systems were limited mainly to knowledgeable users who were comfortable with setting up modems and using text-based terminals. In the 1980s commercial online services began to offer mainstream computer users access to discussion forums, e-mail, chat rooms, online games, and libraries of free software, or shareware. One of the top companies, CompuServe, had about 380,000 subscribers by 1987; nonetheless, another company, America Online (AOL) would come to dominate the 1990s. AOL pioneered an easy-to-use instant message feature as well as popular multiplayer online games such as the dungeon adventure *Neverwinter Nights*. By 2000 AOL had more than 10 million subscribers.

From ARPANET to the Internet

Although the Internet did not gain prominence until the 1990s, it actually has a history that dates back to the 1960s and the era of the Cold War and the space race. Responding to the widespread shock over the Soviet launch of the first artificial satellite, *Sputnik*, the United States greatly increased its funding for scientific research and education.

The Advanced Research Projects Agency (ARPA), part of the US Department of Defense, was established in 1958. A psychologist from the Massachusetts Institute of Technology (MIT), J.C.R. Licklider, was placed in charge of ARPA's Information Processing Techniques Office (IPTO). Licklider had become very interested in how computers might be used to aid human thinking and communication. He believed that in the future a "man-computer symbiosis"[35] would enable humans and computers to work together to tackle problems that neither could solve alone. He also began to talk to colleagues about the possibilities for users of the newly developed time-sharing systems to share computing resources as well as ideas, establishing what he referred to rather grandiosely as "the Intergalactic Computer network."[36]

Being in charge of the IPTO enabled Licklider to fund research in areas such as artificial intelligence, user interfaces, and a computer network called the ARPANET. The need for a truly universal computer network was becoming acute. Robert Taylor, who succeeded Licklider as the IPTO head, recalled the difficulties of having multiple networks:

> For each of these three terminals, I had three different sets of user commands. So if I was talking online with someone at S.D.C. [System Development Corporation] and I wanted to talk to someone I knew at Berkeley or M.I.T. about this, I had to get up from the S.D.C. terminal, go over and log into the other terminal and get in touch with them.

Computer Crime: The Dark Side of Cyberspace

It was inevitable that criminals would figure out ways to steal information from computer systems. Sometimes the break-in is dramatic, as in 2011–2012 when thousands of data records were stolen from a credit card company and a gaming network. More often, though, information is stolen from poorly secured merchant websites or obtained by tricking users (a process known as *phishing*). Increasingly, information is also being harvested from careless postings made by users of social networking sites such as Facebook.

When personal financial information is compromised, the consequences for the victim can be serious. Having one's credit card information stolen can be a major nuisance, even though the account holder does not normally have to pay for the bogus charges. However, stolen information can also be used to impersonate the victim—a crime known as identity theft. An identity thief cannot only drain existing bank or credit accounts but also apply for new accounts and run up bills in the victim's name. Often the first indication that something is wrong is the arrival of statements or bills, or the discovery that one's credit is suddenly bad. It can take months or even years for victims of identity theft to stop debt-collection efforts and repair their credit.

I said, oh, man, it's obvious what to do: If you have these three terminals, there ought to be one terminal that goes anywhere you want to go where you have interactive computing. That idea is the ARPANET.[37]

The basic idea of the ARPANET (and later the Internet) is called packet switching. A packet is rather like a letter in the postal system.

Just as a letter can have any sort of writing in it as long as it is enclosed in a properly addressed envelope, a data packet can contain any sort of information as long as it begins with a properly formatted address that specifies the destination computer. At the post office, machines scan letters, sort them, and send them to the distribution center nearest their destination. Similarly, designated computers use routing tables to look up the destinations of incoming packets and forward them appropriately.

In 1969 the ARPANET was ready for its first test. The telegraph had as its first message, "What hath God wrought?" The telephone had "Mr. Watson—come here—I want to see you." As recalled by networking expert Leonard Kleinrock, the birth of the Internet was somewhat bland: "The transmission itself was simply to 'login' to SRI [Stanford Research Institute] from UCLA [University of California, Los Angeles]. They succeeded in transmitting the 'l' and the 'o' and then the system crashed! Hence the first message on the Internet was 'lo' as in 'lo and behold!'"[38] They were able to do the full login about an hour later.

Restricted at first to government or military-related computers, ARPANET grew slowly. In 1985, however, the National Science Foundation began to fund a new project to link the computer centers it was funding for a variety of scientific projects. Connections were made using a new protocol, or set of rules, called TCP/IP.

Because this new system could link many existing networks together, it became known as the Internet. By the early 1990s restrictions on use of the network had been lifted, and many schools, businesses, and even individuals began to connect to it. Yet just as PCs were hard to use before the Macintosh and Windows, the Internet too needed a new way to make it accessible to mainstream computer users.

Weaving the World Wide Web

In the late 1980s Tim Berners-Lee, a British physicist at the European Organization for Nuclear Research (known as CERN, from its French acronym), was asked to develop a system that could manage the flood of data and scientific papers needed by the lab's researchers, who used a variety of incompatible computer systems. Trying to get everyone to convert their data to the same format was not practical.

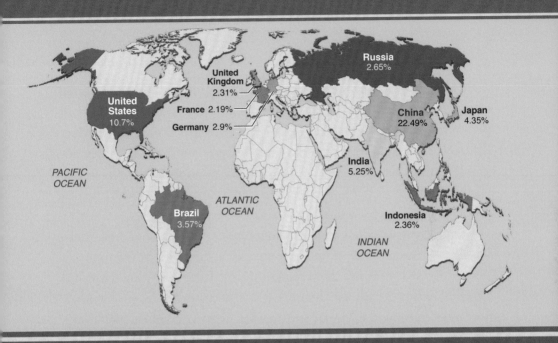

Countries with Largest Share of Total Worldwide Internet Usage, 2012

Russia 2.65%

United Kingdom 2.31%

United States 10.7%

France 2.19%

Germany 2.9%

China 22.49%

Japan 4.35%

India 5.25%

PACIFIC OCEAN

Brazil 3.57%

ATLANTIC OCEAN

Indonesia 2.36%

INDIAN OCEAN

Instead, Berners-Lee built on the existing Internet and its ability to distribute any sort of file to any connected computer. He devised a system in which all pages or documents would be stored on servers connected to the Internet. A user wanting to access a file would use a browser program that would request that item using its unique online address, known as its uniform resource locator (URL). The server would then send the data to the browser, which would display the text on the user's screen. The rules for requesting and sending data would be called the hypertext transfer protocol (HTTP).

If Berners-Lee's system had simply made it easier to retrieve data, it would have been a significant achievement. What made it truly revolutionary was the use of hypertext—the ability to link pages together so the reader could easily explore related ideas. Berners-Lee devised the hypertext markup language (HTML) as a way to create the necessary hypertext. Besides formatting documents, the HTML enables authors to insert a link anywhere and specify what will be retrieved when the reader selects it. Berners-Lee called his system the World Wide Web.

Graphical Browsers

The early World Wide Web did not look very interesting. It consisted mostly of page after page of text, often poorly formatted, and without pictures. One person who was dissatisfied with this situation was Marc Andreessen, a computer scientist and software engineer. In 1993, together with some colleagues at the National Center for Supercomputing Applications (NCSA), Andreessen began working on a web browser that would be graphical and more interactive.

Andreessen recruited another programmer, Eric Bina, and the combination of Andreessen's detailed mastery of coding and Bina's ability to see the big picture made them a good team. Their new browser, called Mosaic, was an instant hit. Because it was developed by a government-funded institution, the Mosaic software was free to download and install. Now pictures from websites could be displayed along with the text, and links could be followed simply by clicking on them with a mouse.

Andreessen believed that a graphical web browser could be combined with new web servers and other software to create business opportunities. Leaving the NCSA, Andreessen and his team built a new browser called Netscape Navigator. Navigator was faster and more attractive than Mosaic, and it also included the secure credit card processing function that was essential for companies wanting to sell goods or services online.

By 1995 Netscape was the leading web browser, but competition soon came from Microsoft and its Internet Explorer. In 2006 another offshoot of Mosaic, called Mozilla, released Firefox, a browser whose attractive features included the ability to add plug-ins to provide for new functions such as playing videos or showing animations. In 2008 Google entered the competition with its Chrome browser, and Apple and other companies also created browsers. By 2012 Internet Explorer and Chrome were about tied in usage share, with Firefox not far behind.

Click to Buy: Amazon and eBay

The new point-and-click browsers, coupled with secure payment systems, made online shopping increasingly attractive. Figuring out what goods or services people would buy, and how to deliver them economically, would be challenging. Two of the biggest early success stories were Amazon and eBay.

Founded by Jeff Bezos in 1994, Amazon began as an online bookstore. In a later interview, Bezos explained how he came up with the name: "Earth's biggest river, Earth's biggest bookstore. . . . Twenty percent of the world's fresh water is in the Amazon River Basin, and we have six times as many titles as the world's largest physical bookstore."[39] Amazon did not become profitable until the end of 2001, but the company's scope and profits both increased dramatically over the next decade. Soon Amazon began to sell music, videos, games, and even clothing—just about anything that could be shipped. In 2011 the company earned $48 billion in revenue.

The other big success story of early e-commerce was eBay, founded in 1995 by Pierre Omidyar, an Iranian American programmer and entrepreneur. eBay brought together people who wanted to sell a variety of items with people who were willing to bid for those items in an auction. eBay caught on very rapidly. In a 2000 article in *GQ* magazine, Omidyar was described as "the . . . King of Stuff [who] created an ingenious mechanism for mining value out of our cluttered, stuff-filled lives, a 'place' where groping buyers and latent sellers could meet and make order (and a few bucks) out of chaos."[40] In 2011 eBay earned $11.6 billion in revenue.

Boom and Bust at the End of the Century

The extraordinary success of Amazon, eBay, PayPal (which developed a secure-payment system for online purchases), and a few other companies encouraged many startup companies to start web-based businesses. Eager speculators often bid up the stock prices of such companies, only to find that their business plans were not always well thought out. In the late 1990s, for instance, a company called Webvan tried to do for groceries what Amazon was doing for books. However, Webvan's owners decided to buy their own warehouses and delivery vans rather than work with supermarkets that already had such infrastructure. As a result, their growth could not keep up with their expenses.

The result of such miscalculations was a wave of failed Internet start-ups. According to computer historian Gerard O'Regan, some of the factors causing the Internet bubble to burst were:

Irrational exuberance on the part of investors.

Insatiable appetite for Internet stocks.

A lack of rationality and common sense by all concerned.

Interest in making money rather than building the business first.[41]

Another Internet flop involved the unsuccessful merger of the faltering online service AOL and the media giant Time-Warner. These failures dampened enthusiasm for technology start-ups during the early 2000s, but there was a gradual recovery. If Amazon and eBay represented the first wave of e-commerce, the next wave would be based on the power of a particular kind of software—the Internet search engine.

Search Engines and Web Portals

Graphical web browsers made it easy to browse, or surf, the Internet. However, as the number of websites grew from thousands to millions, it was hard to actually find the particular information one was seeking. In response to this need, developers began to write programs called search engines. A basic search engine automatically and systematically follows the links from page to page and site to site, recording the keywords it finds in an index. When a user types words into the engine, it uses its index to return a list of matching websites.

A different approach for finding information online was to have a number of experts find the best sites in each of many categories and present them in a sort of catalog. This was the approach of web portals,

Thanks to mobile devices such as smart phones and tablets, users can get driving directions, check bus schedules, search for nearby restaurants or stores, or even participate in games or social networks that focus on one's particular neighborhood. Shoppers can zero in on nearby stores that carry an item and perform automatic price comparisons. Services now in development will allow stores to recognize the faces of their customers and send sale information or coupons directly to their phones.

Like the tracking done by websites, location-aware software on phones can offer marketers more effective advertising while also luring consumers with personalized opportunities. However, software that knows not only what one is doing but where one is doing it raises privacy concerns. Both Google and Apple have been questioned about storing data about users' movements, sometimes over a period of months. Governments could also use location data to track protesters. Vulnerable people, such as residents of battered women's shelters, could also be at risk. It is likely to be some time before legal systems or public policy can catch up with the question of how much control people should have over information about their location, how long such information can be retained, and who should have access to it.

the most successful of which was Yahoo!, which was founded in 1995 by electrical engineering graduates David Filo and Jerry Yang. The drawback of portals was that they were limited to the categories and sites chosen by the developers, and they required considerable effort to keep up to date. Since the 1990s, portals have become less popular as users have become accustomed to the greater flexibility and power of search engines such as Google.

Google: From Search Engine to Web Services

Today the dominant way to find things on the Internet is to use Google, the much more sophisticated search engine developed by Larry Page and Sergey Brin in 1996. Searching for a thesis project, computer-science graduate student Page later recalled that one night he had a rather odd dream: "When I suddenly woke up, I was thinking: what if we could download the whole web, and just keep the links and . . . I grabbed a pen and started writing! Sometimes it is important to wake up and stop dreaming. I spent the middle of that night scribbling out the details and convincing myself it would work."[42]

Page and Brin hit on the idea of examining back links, which are the pages that link to a particular website. Because websites that are considered useful and valuable will have more sites linking to them, the number of back links is a good indication of the quality of a website. After incorporating as Google (and dropping out of school), Page and Brin refined this idea much further, such as by counting not just the number of back links but also the links to the linking sites, and so on.

The other challenge for the new company was how to make money with their new high-quality search engine. Some revenue could come from licensing to sites such as AOL and Yahoo!, which were willing to pay for something that might attract users. However, Page and Brin knew that this end of the business was likely to be limited and temporary. For one thing, increasing numbers of people were simply using the Google site to find what they wanted, bypassing portals like Yahoo!

The key was to combine search results with relevant advertising. Google began selling advertising space through programs such as AdWords and AddSense, which used sophisticated mechanisms to adjust ad prices and placement according to effectiveness. This kind of marketing needed a delicate balance—the ads needed to be noticeable but not obtrusive. Page and Brin also felt strongly that users should always know what listings were the actual search results and what items were paid for, or sponsored. Google's founders were never shy about their ambitions for their search engine, which they viewed as a way to tap into an ever-expanding universe of knowledge. In a recent book about Google, author Steven Levy quotes Brin as saying, "Ultimately I view Google as a way to augment your brain with the knowledge of the world."[43]

Meanwhile, Google expanded rapidly. It acquired a variety of existing web-based services, improved them, and then integrated them into an ever-growing menu that included a leading e-mail provider (Gmail), a set of online office programs (Google Docs), the world's biggest video-sharing site (YouTube), the popular Google Maps and Google Earth, and the Google+ social network. In 2012 Google seemed to be positioning itself to compete with Amazon in selling books, music, and video as well as with Apple by marketing its own tablet computer.

A three-dimensional view of San Francisco can be seen on Google Earth, the digital mapping service created by search engine giant Google. Sifting through millions of websites to find information on the web is impossible. Google and other search engines have greatly simplified such searches.

Social Networks

By the mid-2000s much attention and investment capital had begun to focus on a new kind of web application: the social network. The most successful network has been Facebook, which was founded by Harvard student Mark Zuckerberg in 2004. Like Google, Facebook started as a campus-based project—an attempt to create an electronic version of

Social networks such as Facebook, represented by the lower case "f" on a blue background, have become a huge part of daily life for people around the world. Such networks allow people to connect with friends and others who share common interests regardless of where they live or time of day.

the "face" books that traditionally included students' photos, contact information, and interests. Less than a decade later, Facebook could count about 600 million users worldwide.

According to technology writer Fred Vogelstein, Facebook represents an alternative to Google's vision of how the Internet should be organized and used: "Zuckerberg envisions a more personalized, humanized Web, where our network of friends, colleagues, peers, and family is our primary source of information, just as it is offline. In Zuckerberg's vision, users will query this 'social graph' to find a doctor, the best camera, or someone to hire—rather than tapping the cold mathematics of a Google search."[44]

Another popular social networking site, Twitter, stripped the idea of Facebook down to its essentials—people talking about what they are doing. Using short messages delivered in real time, Twitter soon built on the popular online activity of blogging, or posting an online journal of one's opinions, activities, or interests. Created in 2006 by online entrepreneur Jack Dorsey, Twitter had about 500 million active users in 2012, posting 340 million messages (called tweets) each day.

Social networks have thus become a major part of the daily life of many people. They post frequent Facebook or Google+ updates describing weddings, graduations, vacation trips, parties, or other social events. Photos can be shared on sites such as Flickr or Picasa. Meanwhile, of course, people are constantly checking for their friends' latest postings and commenting on them. For keeping in touch with things as they happen, the immediacy of Twitter's text messages can be attractive.

Mobile Devices: Always Connected

Since the 1990s, thanks in part to the usefulness of Google and other services, computers have become a part of daily life. They also have morphed into a variety of handy devices, some small enough to fit comfortably in one's pocket. Originally called personal digital assistants (PDAs), the most successful of these early devices was the Palm Pilot, which could replace an address book or calendar, serve as a notebook, and (with later versions) send e-mail.

Meanwhile, cell phones, which had started out as brick-sized devices, were also becoming popular by the 1990s. Combining the organizational features of a PDA with the ability to make phone calls, the BlackBerry (first released in 1999) became wildly popular with businesspeople. The next step in this line of evolution involved creating phones with larger, higher resolution displays as well as enough memory and a fast enough processor to host a complete operating system and run applications (better known as *apps*).

In 2007 Apple, which had already revolutionized the mobile music market with its iPod, released its first iPhone. This wildly successful device and its successors, together with a number of competitors, feature a touch-screen interface and the ability not only to communicate via phone, text messages, or e-mail but also to play music, show videos, and run thousands of programs, including many popular games. Writing for *Time* magazine in 2012, Richard Stengel declared,

> The mobile phone has become a kind of super extension of ourselves—faster, brainier, more reliable and always on. . . . There are now more smart phones than toilets in many parts of the world, and the average smart phone today has more computing power than Apollo 11 did when it journeyed to the moon.[45]

Thus, through ingenious devices and ever-expanding applications, the digital age had penetrated virtually every aspect of daily life by the early twenty-first century.

Chapter 5

What Is the Legacy of the Digital Age?

The digital age is far from over. In its early stages it was characterized by rapid change and surprising developments. It continues in this fashion, influencing daily life on a global scale, offering new opportunities, and raising many challenges for future generations.

Business and Work in a Connected World

The widespread use of Google, mobile devices, and social networks has made it necessary for just about every business to pay attention to how it is found or perceived online. Even a small neighborhood restaurant wants to appear on Google maps and fears getting negative customer reviews on a site such as Yelp.

Corporations and professionals like doctors and lawyers must now be concerned about their reputations as influenced by what people can find about them online. Companies such as ReputationDefender have even sprung up to help monitor the online presence of their clients. These companies will ask websites to take down offending items and then counter them with a flood of positive postings.

Meanwhile, both job seekers and existing employees must also be concerned about their online reputations. Recently some individuals have lost jobs (or not been offered them) because employers were concerned about something they had posted online—for example, a video showing drunken antics at a party perhaps years ago. Some employers have required that applicants give them the password to their Facebook page so they can monitor it. This has led to calls to protect privacy by banning such requirements.

New Forms of Collaboration

Even as it raises new challenges for employers and workers, today's online world offers innovative ways to organize projects. By far the most prominent example of an open collaborative project today is Wikipedia. Traditional encyclopedias were written over a long period by recognized experts and then were carefully edited but infrequently updated. Wikipedia is written and edited by users under community-enforced standards. In 2012 Wikipedia had nearly 4 million articles in English alone. Various forms of wiki software are also used in many corporations and schools to create specialized or local bodies of knowledge.

The philosophy of open collaboration has led to a more general approach to problem solving. Known as crowd sourcing, the basic idea is to let people join together online to tackle a problem. Sometimes this simply involves people allowing their computers to spend part of their otherwise idle time analyzing potential extraterrestrial signals (SETI@Home) or computing the configuration of proteins (Folding@Home). People can, after brief training, be given photographs or microscope slides in order to identify, for example, drug-resistant tuberculosis cells—tasks that are still quite difficult for current artificial intelligence systems.

Another form of online collaboration involves a recent development known as crowd funding. Through sites such as Kickstarter, an idea or project can be offered for collaboration with the agreement to proceed with development if enough money is pledged. For example, two recent documentary films, *Sun Come Up* and *Incident in New Baghdad*, were funded through Kickstarter and were later nominated for the Academy Award.

New Vulnerabilities

The services that bring people together for new forms of work and relationships also bring threats to privacy and personal security. Such threats are hard to counter because they are a direct consequence of always being

The digital age has resulted in new forms of online collaboration. The SETI@Home project, for instance, involves people around the globe who allow their Internet-connected computers to analyze radio telescope signals as part of a scientific search for extraterrestrial life.

connected to everyone, or everything, everywhere. The same access that allows for so many innovative applications in business and social networking also provides tools for criminals, foreign enemies, and terrorists.

Many web users are now aware of the "cookies" and other devices used by marketers to track what people do on the Internet. A study by the *Wall Street Journal* found that the top fifty American websites installed an average of sixty-four pieces of tracking technology, usually without notifying users. Many of these are cookies, but newer technology includes "beacons" that can track what a user is doing in real time and correlate it with the user's location and demographics. The information thus gathered is not only being packaged and sold to marketers, it is even being auctioned in real time.

Tracking technology is now also widely used with mobile devices. In 2011 it was revealed that a company called Carrier IQ had installed

Apps and the Cloud

Until recently most computer users would agree that operating systems control the computer, and application programs enable it to do useful things. The Internet is a good place to find information and to communicate with other people, but to create a document or spreadsheet, one needed to install software. Likewise, any important data needed to be backed up to a local drive.

All of these assumptions have recently been brought into question. Many applications are now run directly from the Internet, using facilities such as Google Docs. Even the operating system can largely be dispensed with, as in Google's Chrome OS, which provides a desktop and file system directly through the browser. The new buzzword is *the Cloud*, referring to providing applications and storing user data on a network of servers, not the local PC. This approach means that users can work with the same data on many different devices—at a desk at work, a laptop or tablet in a café or on a plane, and even using a smart phone.

The Cloud offers an increasing number of computer users the ability to access data from any connected device at any time. Data is automatically kept up to date and backed up, safe from disk failure, fire, theft, or other mishaps. However, the dependability of the Cloud provider then becomes an issue. There are also concerns about privacy and protection of the stored data from criminal intruders.

tracking software on more than 150 million cell phones. While the company said this data was only used to monitor network performance, the fact that the tracking was done without users' knowledge is disturbing.

The spread of popular phone apps also offers new opportunities for data tracking. Most apps are free or cost only a few dollars. But one phone carrier executive was quoted as saying, "No app is free. You pay for them with your privacy."[46]

Threats to privacy, the danger of computer viruses and malware, and the prospect of identity theft would seem to be enough for most individuals to worry about. However, there are also the large-scale threats of online espionage, sabotage, and even cyberwar and cyberterrorism. According to a recent FBI analysis, more than one hundred nations have intelligence agencies with such capabilities. The low cost of hardware (the software is mostly free) puts these techniques well within the reach of organized criminals and terrorist groups.

In 2010 it was discovered that the Stuxnet computer worm had apparently been used to spin Iran's uranium enrichment centrifuges out of control. This incident highlights the fact that banking and credit card systems are not the only targets of cyberattacks—even electrical power grids are susceptible. This, in turn, raises the issue of how to protect vital facilities without hampering the free flow of information online or invading the privacy of people's e-mail and other activities.

Lifelong Learning and the Virtual Classroom

How can ordinary computer users cope with the sophisticated threats and issues raised by the digital age? Both basic education and ongoing, life-long training are required. Fortunately, the technology whose complexity poses challenges to educators also offers powerful resources for teaching. When computers first began to appear in classrooms during the 1980s, the emphasis was on using software to assess students' skills in subjects such as math and reading and to provide opportunities for drill and practice. However, creative educators also began to use computer games and simulations to teach science, social studies, and other subjects. It is one thing to read about urban problems in a textbook, but another to actually try to design and run one's own metropolis in the *SimCity* game.

Today the emphasis is shifting to using the computer as a tool for research and collaboration. Many classes have websites or Facebook pages. Students are encouraged to create blogs or join with others to create a wiki on a subject or theme. In other words, students are using many of the same tools and services as adults.

As with other aspects of the digital age, the benefits of students' being online come with concerns. The issue of online harassment, often termed *cyberbullying*, has sometimes had tragic or even fatal consequences. The ease and fluency many young people have in using new social technology is not always matched by the knowledge and psychological maturity needed to respond appropriately to bullies or online predators.

Just as the line between what is educational and what is social is blurring, the walls of the classroom are beginning to dissolve. Colleges and even a few high schools now conduct their classes online, and one can get a degree from a reputable university without leaving one's computer.

Media's Endless Stream

Much of society's experience of digital technology is not through school or work but rather as a form of entertainment. One of the most noticeable trends of the recent digital age has been a rapid change in how people use media, whether printed books or newspapers, music, video, or television programs. Formerly, each kind of media was delivered by a separate provider and was consumed using a different device. Thus, one might read a newspaper, go to the library for a book, play a record, or watch a television show.

Today a single device—a desktop or laptop computer, tablet, or smart phone—can be used to read print media, listen to music, or watch video. This change in how media is delivered has been a major challenge to book publishers, newspapers, record companies, and even television networks. Instead of having sole control over how their products are priced and marketed, they must now negotiate with Amazon, Google, Apple, and other companies that sell directly online.

The fact that music and books can now come directly to consumers is also changing how musicians and writers get paid for their work. For example, bands that used to make much of their money from selling CDs may now distribute their music directly through downloads. They

Media consumption has undergone dramatic changes in the digital age. Advances have made it possible to get news, listen to music, watch a movie, read a book, and even carry on a conversation with a single device.

now may get less for their music, so they focus instead on selling concert tickets and merchandise.

The challenge for journalists and newspapers is a bit different but is also forcing them to find new ways to operate. Traditional print media have largely depended on revenue from advertising. However, online advertising services (particularly Google) are growing rapidly. Faced with a loss of revenue, newspapers have attempted to create online sites and apps with special features to attract subscribers willing to pay to read their content online.

Digital Government and Politics

Today no government leader or political candidate can afford to ignore the reality of the Internet and the new forms of communication and

Ultimate Intelligence?

Recently an IBM artificial intelligence (AI) program called Watson defeated the best human contestants in the quiz program *Jeopardy*. Given the nuances of language and culture required to master *Jeopardy*, this achievement suggests that AI programs are beginning to gain the general-purpose versatility of human minds. Meanwhile, Apple's 2011 iPhone 4S introduced Siri, a voice-activated personal assistant that, although not perfect, often shows a remarkable ability to understand real-life requests.

Prolific inventor and futurist Ray Kurzweil has suggested that by the mid-twenty-first century the development of advanced AI and robotics, combined with advances in human brain science and genetic engineering, will create a future as incomprehensible as the inside of a black hole. In his book *The Singularity Is Near*, Kurzweil refers to the "Singularity" as "a future period during which the pace of technological change will be so rapid, its impact so deep, that human life will be irreversibly transformed."

Critics of AI have pointed out since the 1950s that human-level artificial intelligence always seems to be only a decade or two away. The impressive feats of a Watson perhaps owe more to clever algorithms and brute force calculations and statistical analysis than to human-style thought. Nevertheless, it can be argued that human life has already been "irreversibly transformed" by the digital age.

Ray Kurzweil, *The Singularity Is Near: When Humans Transcend Biology*. New York: Viking, 2005, p. 7.

expression that it makes possible. A particular issue is the accountability of both officeholders and candidates to the public. Citizens and journalists increasingly expect government agencies to put their records and reports online. However, the degree of transparency and accessibility of data varies considerably. For example, despite the widespread interest in the influence of campaign contributions and so-called independent expenditures on politics, it can be hard for voters to determine exactly who is behind a particular candidate or ballot measure. Gradually this problem is being addressed by such sites as opensecrets.org, which compiles and summarizes information about campaign contributions and lobbying efforts.

The widespread availability of connected devices also poses challenges on the campaign trail. With cell phones functioning as pocket-size video cameras and sound recorders, any off-color remark or rash promise made by a politician in a supposedly private gathering is likely to be all over the Internet in a matter of hours. Bloggers, often acting as citizen journalists, sometimes unearth and break stories that the established media is slow or reluctant to pursue. For example, in 2002 Senator Trent Lott of Mississippi praised the career of South Carolina senator Strom Thurmond, who had supported racial segregation during the 1950s and 1960s. Although Lott's remarks were only briefly reported in the mainstream media, bloggers kept the issue in the spotlight. Lott was forced to step down from his post as Republican Senate leader.

By 2012 social networking had gone from being a novelty or sideline to being an integral part of every campaign from president down to city councillor. Every campaign has a website, most have blogs, and many have Twitter feeds so supporters can follow them and be kept up to date. Increasingly, major campaigns (such as those of presidential candidates Barack Obama and Mitt Romney in 2012) are creating phone apps that provide additional ways to connect to supporters. Sometimes a campaign donation can be made simply by clicking and sending a text message. Campaigns are also adopting many of the techniques used by advertisers, targeting their messages to people according to their location and interests.

The political importance of social networks and mobile services thus seems to be growing. According to the 2012 survey "Politics on Social Networking Sites," conducted by the Pew Internet and American Life Project, social networks are becoming important conduits for political action and information. According to the survey, 36 percent of respondents believe that social networks are important or somewhat important for obtaining relevant news. About 25 percent consider social networks to be useful for recruiting supporters, finding people who share their views, or conducting debates or discussions.

Social Movements and Activism

Around the world, from the Arab Spring revolutions in 2011 against oppressive governments in Egypt, Tunisia, and other countries to the Occupy Wall Street protests against economic inequality in the United States, digital technology has played a part. Facebook, Twitter, and other online tools have been used to coordinate protests and document clashes with police. In Egypt a Facebook page protesting police brutality and torture used a feature more commonly used to announce parties to disseminate instructions for people planning to take part in public demonstrations. One of the protest organizers instructed: "Stand 5 feet apart, so as not to break Egyptian laws against public demonstration; be absolutely silent; no signs; wear black, as determined in an online vote; stand on the banks of the river or sea for one hour only, then walk away."[47]

Even when governments attempt to censor or shut down online access, pictures and videos have a way of surfacing. This makes social media a powerful tool for activists—both liberal and conservative. During the 2012 Egyptian elections, the conservative religious group known as the Muslim Brotherhood organized a massive and successful campaign on Twitter.

Online activism has sometimes gone beyond protest to the use of more controversial tactics. For example, the shadowy online group called Anonymous supported and helped organize the largely peaceful demonstrations during the Occupy Wall Street movement of 2011–2012. However, hackers identifying themselves with the group shut down several federal and corporate websites in early 2012 to protest pending federal legislation that they viewed as an attack on the free use of the Internet. Meanwhile, another shadowy group called Wikileaks obtained and posted online thousands of confidential US diplomatic messages as well as reports of military activities.

Egyptian protesters use cell phones to record the momentous events taking place in Cairo's Tahrir Square in 2011. Social networks such as Twitter and Facebook and cell phone recorders and cameras have become essential tools in social movements around the world.

Supporters of Anonymous and Wikileaks see themselves as forces for making government more accountable by piercing the veil of secrecy. Opponents argue that these "hacktivist" groups are themselves unaccountable, and their actions could endanger national security and delicate foreign negotiations.

The ultimate value of using digital-age tools to promote social change is also being debated. Journalist and essayist Malcolm Gladwell has argued that the technology can create only "weak ties"—casual connections rather than the strong commitments that might arise from individuals working together in person. Gladwell believes that weak ties cannot foster the kind of committed, courageous activism that typified, for example, the American civil rights movement of the 1950s and 1960s:

> Our acquaintances—not our friends—are our greatest source of new ideas and information. The Internet lets us exploit the power of these kinds of distant connections with marvelous efficiency. It's terrific at the diffusion of innovation, interdisciplinary collaboration, seamlessly matching up buyers and sellers, and the logistical functions of the dating world. But weak ties seldom lead to high-risk activism.[48]

On the other hand, the ability of social media to let a large number of people do a little can end up doing a lot. Jed Alpert, cofounder and chief executive officer of Mobile Commons and an online social and political consultant, suggests that organizations such as the Red Cross could increase donations and volunteer activity by Google-style targeting. "What if you sent $10 to a food bank via text and received a return text suggesting a local soup kitchen—chosen on the basis of your area code—where you could volunteer this weekend?"[49]

Being Human in the Digital Age

Perhaps the most profound legacy of the digital age is what it is doing to the whole experience of being human. What does it mean to be a *self* when one can have many different online identities? What about the balance between one's inner life and the demands of social interaction? In the essay "The End of Solitude," social commentator William Deresiewicz notes:

> A constant stream of mediated contact, virtual, notional, or simulated, keeps us wired in to the electronic hive—though contact, or at least two-way contact, seems increasingly beside the point. The goal now, it seems, is simply to become known, to turn oneself into a sort of miniature celebrity. How many friends do I have on Facebook? How many people are reading my blog? How many Google hits does my name generate?

Visibility secures our self-esteem, becoming a substitute, twice removed, for genuine connection. Not long ago, it was easy to feel lonely. Now, it is impossible to be alone.[50]

Indeed, the pull of being always on seems relentless. In the 2012 "Mobility Poll," *Time* magazine and the telecommunications company Qualcomm surveyed cell phone users in the United States and seven other countries. According to the poll, one in four users checks his or her phone every thirty minutes, and one in five does so every ten minutes. One-third of users said that being without their phone for even a short time made them feel anxious. Three-quarters of twenty-five- to twenty-nine-year-olds said they even sleep with their phones.

The new technology thus brings people together in new ways, such as by ending the isolation of some senior citizens or people in remote communities. At the same time, it may be splitting people off from themselves. A new way of being may be emerging, with consequences that require thoughtful consideration.

Source Notes

Introduction: The Defining Characteristics of the Digital Age

1. Quoted in Randy Alfred, "Aug. 9, 1854: Thoreau Warns, the Railroad Rides on Us," *Wired: This Day in Tech*. www.wired.com.

2. Nathaniel Hawthorne, *The House of the Seven Gables*. Project Gutenberg. www.gutenberg.org.

3. Neil Postman, "Five Things We Need to Know About Technological Change." Address to the New Tech 98 Conference, Denver, CO, March 27, 1998. www.mat.upm.es.

4. Quoted in Ray Kurzweil, *The Singularity Is Near: When Humans Transcend Biology*. New York: Viking, 2005, p. 22.

5. Kevin Kelly, *What Technology Wants*. New York: Viking, p. 15.

Chapter One: What Conditions Led to the Digital Age?

6. Quoted in Maurice Wilkes, "Babbage's Expectations for His Engines," *Annals of the History of Computing*, 1991, vol. 13, pp. 141–45.

7. Quoted in Robert Slater, *Portraits in Silicon*. Cambridge, MA: MIT Press, 1987, p. 35.

8. Quoted in "Retiring Computer Pioneer—Anthony G. Oettinger, Howard Aiken," *Communications of the Association for Computing Machinery*, June 1962, p. 298–99.

9. Quoted in Lars Nielsen, *Computing: A Business History*. Wickford, RI: New Street Communications, 2011.

10. Quoted in S. Augarten, *Bit by Bit: An Illustrated History of Computers*. New York: Ticknor & Fields, 1984, p. 99.

11. A.M. Turing, "Computing Machinery and Intelligence," Loebner Prize in Artificial Intelligence. www.loebner.net.

12. C. Dianne Martin, "ENIAC: The Press Conference That Shook the World," *IEEE Technology and Society Magazine*, December 1995, p. 7.

13. James C. McPherson, "Census Experience Operating a UNIVAC System," Symposium on Managerial Aspects of Digital Computer Installations, Washington, DC, March 30, 1953.

14. Roddy Osborn, "GE and UNIVAC: Harnessing the High-Speed Computer," *Harvard Business Review*, July/August 1954, pp. 99–107.

15. Quoted in Brian Hayes, "Automation on the Job: Computers Were Supposed to Be Labor-Saving Devices. How Come We're Still Working So Hard?," *American Scientist*, January/February 2009. www.americanscientist.org.

16. Norbert Wiener, *The Human Use of Human Beings*. Boston: Houghton Mifflin, 1954, p. 162.

17. Quoted in Hayes, "Automation on the Job."

Chapter Two: Mighty Mainframes

18. Quoted in Nielsen, *Computing*.

19. Quoted in Slater, *Portraits in Silicon,* p. 108.

20. Quoted in Nicholas Metropolis, *A History of Computing in the Twentieth Century*. New York: Academic, 1980, p. 126.

21. Quoted in Slater, *Portraits in Silicon*, p. 233.

22. Quoted in Draper Prize, "1993 Winner: John W. Backus." www.draperprize.org.

23. Quoted in Slater, *Portraits in Silicon*, p. 225.

Chapter Three: Computers Get Personal

24. Quoted in Slater, *Portraits in Silicon*, p. 179.

25. Quoted in Stephen Wozniak, "Homebrew and How the Apple Came to Be," AtariArchives.org. www.atariarchives.org.

26. Bill Gates, "An Open Letter to Hobbyists," *Homebrew Computer Club Newsletter*, January 31, 1976, p. 2.

27. Slater, *Portraits in Silicon*, p. 313.

28. *Time,* "The Computer Moves In," January 3, 1983, pp. 14–28.

29. Quoted in Wayne Carlson, "A Critical History of Computer Graphics and Animation," Ohio State University. http://design.osu.edu.

30. Apple Macintosh commercial, 1984. http://video.google.com/video play?docid=-715862862672743260.

31. Quoted in Nielsen, *Computing*.

32. Quoted in Academy of Achievement, "William H. Gates III." www .achievement.org.

Chapter Four: A Connected World

33. Quoted in Jeffrey M. Tobias, ed., *Language Design and Programming Methodology*. New York: Springer, 1980, p. 1.

34. Quoted in Michael Hauben and Ronda Hauben, *Netizens: On the History and Impact of Usenet and the Internet*. www.columbia.edu.

35. J.C.R. Licklider, "Man-Computer Symbiosis," *IRE Transactions on Human Factors in Electronics*, March 1960, vol. HFE-1, pp. 4–11. http://groups.csail.mit.edu.

36. J.C.R. Licklider, "Memorandum for Members and Affiliates of the Intergalactic Computer Network," April 23, 1963, Kurzweil Accelerating Intelligence. www.kurzweilai.net.

37. John Markoff, "An Internet Pioneer Ponders the Next Revolution," *New York Times*, December 20, 1999. http://partners.nytimes.com.

38. Leonard Kleinrock, "The Day the Infant Internet Uttered Its First Words," University of California, Los Angeles. www.lk.cs.ucla.edu.

39. Quoted in Karen Southwick, "Interview with Jeff Bezos of Amazon .com," *Upside*, October 1996, pp. 29–34.

40. Adam Sachs, "The Billionaire No One Knows," *GQ*, May 2000, p. 235.

41. Gerard O'Regan, *A Brief History of Computing*, 2nd ed. New York: Springer, 2008, p. 113.

42. *News from Google* (blog), "Larry Page's University of Michigan Commencement Address," May 2, 2009. www.google.com.

43. Quoted in Steven Levy, *In the Plex: How Google Thinks, Works, and Shapes Our Lives*. New York: Simon & Schuster, 2011, p. 67.

44. Fred Vogelstein, "Great Wall of Facebook: The Social Network's Plan to Dominate the Internet—and Keep Google Out," *Wired*, July 2009. www.wired.com.

45. Richard Stengel, editorial, *Time*, August 27, 2012, p. 4.

Chapter Five: What Is the Legacy of the Digital Age?

46. Quoted in Massimo Calabresi, "The Phone Knows All," *Time*, August 27, 2012, p. 31.

47. John D. Sutter, "The Faces of Egypt's 'Revolution 2.0,'" CNN Tech, February 1, 2011. www.cnn.com.

48. Malcolm Gladwell, "Small Change: Why the Revolution Will Not Be Tweeted," *New Yorker*, October 4, 2010. www.newyorker.com.

49. Quoted in Kate Pickert, "Doing Good by Texting," *Time*, August 27, 2012, p. 27.

50. William Deresiewicz, "The End of Solitude," *Chronicle Review*, January 30, 2009. http://chronicle.com.

Important People of the Digital Age

John Backus: Developed the high-level computer language compiler FORTRAN.

Tim Berners-Lee: Devised the World Wide Web to allow uniform access and linkage to documents over the Internet.

Jeff Bezos: Founder of Amazon, one of the most successful web-based companies.

J. Presper Eckert and John Mauchly: Constructed ENIAC, one of the first programmable electronic digital computers.

Bill Gates: As cofounder and chief executive officer of Microsoft, he established Windows as the principal PC operating system and developed leading office software and other dominant products.

Grace Hopper: Developed the high-level computer language compiler COBOL.

Steve Jobs: The cofounder and CEO of Apple; he was largely responsible for the distinctive style and user-friendly design associated with Apple's Macintosh and mobile products.

J.C.R. Licklider: Researched human-computer interaction and networking; provided much of the leadership in developing what would become the Internet.

Pierre Omidyar: Founder of eBay, one of the most sucessful web-based companies.

Larry Page and Sergey Brin: As the founders of Google, they turned a sophisticated search engine into a wide-ranging array of services.

Alan Turing: Developed the theory of the universal computer, played a major role in the British World War II code-breaking effort, and pioneered the exploration of machine intelligence.

John von Neumann: Formulated and advanced the basic architecture of the digital computer, including the ability of the machine to store its own programs

Thomas J. Watson Sr.: Led IBM from mechanical office machines to the development of industry-leading mainframe computers.

For Further Research

Books

Ken Auletta, *Googled: The End of the World as We Know It*. New York: Penguin, 2009.

Tim Berners-Lee, *Weaving the Web*. San Francisco: HarperSanFrancisco, 1999.

Paul Freiberger and Michael Swaine, *Fire in the Valley: The Making of the Personal Computer*. 2nd ed. New York: McGraw-Hill, 2000.

Harry Henderson, *Encyclopedia of Computer Science and Technology*. Rev. ed. New York: Facts On File, 2009.

Andy Herzfeld, *Revolution in the Valley: The Insanely Great Story of How the Mac Was Made*. Sebastapol, CA: O'Reilly, 2005.

Walter Isaacson, *Steve Jobs*. New York: Simon & Schuster, 2011.

Kevin Kelly, *What Technology Wants*. New York: Viking, 2010.

David Kirkpatrick, *The Facebook Effect: The Inside Story of the Company That Is Connecting the World*. New York: Simon & Schuster, 2010.

Steven Levy, *Hackers: Heroes of the Computer Revolution*. Sebastapol, CA: O'Reilly, 2010.

Gerard O'Regan, *A Brief History of Computing*. 2nd ed. New York: Springer, 2012.

Ian Watson, *The Universal Machine: From the Dawn of Computing to Digital Consciousness*. New York: Copernicus, 2012.

Websites

Association for Computing Machinery (www.acm.org). This leading computer-science organization offers resources for people interested in careers in computing as well as historical information about the field.

"Computer History," Computer Hope (www.computerhope.com). This site provides detailed timelines and descriptions of many "firsts" (some controversial) in computer history.

Computer History Museum (www.computerhistory.org). This museum website showcases both physical and online exhibits and provides fascinating facts about the development of computers.

NetHistory (www.nethistory.info). This site offers a trove of historical documents and commentary relating to the development of many aspects of the Internet.

Pew Internet and American Life Project (http://pewinternet.org). This organization conducts regular surveys and analysis of many aspects of how digital technology is being adopted and used by different groups of people.

Search Engine Watch (http://searchenginewatch.com). A comprehensive source for news and statistics on search engines, online advertising, and related e-commerce developments.

Social Networking Watch (www.socialnetworkingwatch.com). A good site for news and trends involving social networking sites and applications.

ZDNet: (www.zdnet.com). A comprehensive site for computer industry news and product reviews.

Index

Note: Boldface page numbers indicate illustrations.

Picture Credits

About the Author

Harry Henderson has written more than thirty books on science and technology, particularly computing. He lives with his wife, Lisa Yount (a retired writer and active artist), in El Cerrito, California.